# A HILLTOP ON
# THE MARNE

The House on the Hill.

# A HILLTOP ON THE MARNE

BY

MILDRED ALDRICH

LONDON
CONSTABLE AND COMPANY LTD.
1915

*0354*

*Copyright* 1915
*by*
*Mildrea Aldrich*

£000100310

PRINTED IN GREAT BRITAIN.
CHISWICK PRESS: CHARLES WHITTINGHAM AND CO.
TOOKS COURT, CHANCERY LANE  LONDON.

# A HILLTOP ON THE MARNE

## I

*June* 3, 1914.

WELL, the deed is done. I have not wanted to talk with you much about it until I was here. I know all your objections. You remember that you did not spare me when, a year ago, I told you that this was my plan. I realize that you—more active, younger, more interested in life, less burdened with your past—feel that it is cowardly on my part to seek a quiet refuge and settle myself into it, to turn my face peacefully to the exit, feeling that the end is the most interesting event ahead of me—the one truly interesting experience left to me in this incarnation.

I am not proposing to ask you to see it from my point of view. You cannot, no matter how willing you are to try. No two people ever see life from the same angle. There is a law which decrees that two objects may not occupy the same place at the same time—result, two people cannot see things from the same point of view, and the slightest difference in angle changes the thing seen.

I did not decide to come away into a little

5

corner in the country, in this land in which I was not born, without looking at the move from all angles. Be sure that I know what I am doing, and I have found the place where I can do it. Some time you will see the new home, I hope, and then you will understand. I have lived more than sixty years. I have lived a fairly active life, and it has been, with all its hardships—and they have been many—interesting. But I have had enough of the city—even of Paris, the most beautiful city in the world. Nothing can take any of that away from me. It is treasured up in my memory. I am even prepared to own that there was a sort of arrogance in my persistence in choosing for so many years the most seduct- ive city in the world, and saying, "Let others live where they will—here I propose to stay." I lived there until I seemed to take it for my own—to know it on the surface and under it, and over it, and around it; until I had a sort of morbid jealousy when I found any one who knew it half as well as I did, or presumed to love it half as much, and dared to say so. You will please note that I have not gone far from it.

But I have come to feel the need of calm and quiet—perfect peace. I know again that there is a sort of arrogance in expecting it, but I am going to make a bold bid for it. I will agree, if you like, that it is cowardly to say that my work is done. I will even agree that we both know plenty of women who have cheerfully gone on struggling to a far greater age, and I do think it downright pretty of you to find me younger than my years. Yet you must forgive me if I say that none of us know one another, and, likewise, that appearances are often deceptive.

What you are pleased to call my " pride " has helped me a little. No one can decide for another the proper moment for striking one's colours.

I am sure that you—or for that matter any other American—never heard of Huiry. Yet it is a little hamlet, less than thirty miles from Paris. It is in that district between Paris and Meaux little known to the ordinary traveller. It only consists of less than a dozen rude farm-houses, less than five miles, as the bird flies, from Meaux, which, with a fair cathedral, and a beautiful chestnut-shaded promenade on the banks of the Marne, spanned just there by lines of old mills whose water-wheels churn the river into foaming eddies, has never been popular with excursionists. There are people who go there to see where Bossuet wrote his funeral orations, in a little summer-house standing among pines and cedars on the wall of the garden of the Archbishop's palace, now, since the " separation," the property of the State, and soon to be a town museum. It is not a very attractive town. It has not even an out-of-doors restaurant to tempt the passing automobilist.

My house was, when I leased it, little more

than a peasant's hut. It is considerably over
one hundred and fifty years old, with stables
and outbuildings attached whimsically, and
boasts six gables. Is it not a pity, for early
association's sake, that it has not one more?

I have, as Traddles used to say, "Oceans of
room, Copperfield," and no joking. I have on
the ground floor of the main building a fair
sized salon, into which the front door opens
directly. Over that I have a long, narrow bedroom and dressing-room, and above that, in the
eaves, a sort of attic workshop. In an attached,
one-storey addition with a gable, at the west of
the salon, I have a library lighted from both
east and west. Behind the salon, on the west
side, I have a double room which serves as din-
ing- and breakfast-room, with a guest-chamber
above. The kitchen, at the north side of the
salon, has its own gable, and there is an old
stable extending forward at the north side, and
an old grange extending west from the dining-
room. It is a jumble of roofs and chimneys,
and looks very much like the houses I used to
combine from my Noah's Ark box in the days
of my babyhood.

All the rooms on the ground floor are paved
in red tiles, and the staircase is built right in
the salon. The ceilings are raftered. The cross-
beam in the salon fills my soul with joy—it is
over a foot wide and a foot and a half thick.
The walls and the rafters are painted green,—

my colour,—and so good, by long trial, for my eyes and my nerves, and my disposition.

But much as I like all this, it was not this that attracted me here. That was the situation. The house stands in a small garden, separated from the road by an old gnarled hedge of hazel. It is almost on the crest of the hill on the south bank of the Marne—the hill that is the watershed between the Marne and the Grand Morin. Just here the Marne makes a wonderful loop, and is only fifteen minutes' walk away from my gate, down the hill to the north.

From the lawn, on the north side of the house, I command a panorama which I have rarely seen equalled. To me it is more beautiful than that we have so often looked at together from the terrace at St. Germain. In the west the new part of Esbly climbs the hill, and from there to a hill at the north-east I have a wide view of the valley of the Marne, backed by a low line of hills which is the water-shed between the Marne and the Aisne. Low down in the valley, at the north-west, lies Ile de Villenoy, like a toy town, where the big bridge spans the Marne to carry the railroad into Meaux. On the horizon line to the west the tall chimneys of Claye send lines of smoke into the air. In the foreground to the north, at the foot of the hill, are the roofs of two little hamlets,—Joncheroy and Voisins,—and beyond them the trees that border the canal.

# A HILLTOP ON THE MARNE

On the other side of the Marne the undulating hill, with its wide stretch of fields, is dotted with little villages that peep out of the trees or are silhouetted against the sky-line,—Vignely, Trilbardou, Penchard, Monthyon, Neufmortier, Chauconin, and in the foreground to the north, in the valley, just halfway between me and Meaux, lies Mareuil-on-the-Marne, with its red roofs, gray walls, and church spire. With a glass I can find where Chambry and Barcy are, on the slope behind Meaux, even if the trees conceal them.

But these are all little villages of which you may never have heard. No guide-book celebrates them. No railroad approaches them. On clear days I can see the square tower of the cathedral at Meaux, and I have only to walk a short distance on the *route nationale*,—which runs from Paris, across the top of my hill a little to the east, and thence to Meaux and on to the frontier,—to get a profile view of it standing up above the town, quite detached, from foundation to clock-tower.

This is a rolling country of grain fields, orchards, masses of black-currant bushes, vegetable plots,—it is a great sugar-beet country,— and asparagus beds; for the Department of the Seine et Marne is one of the most productive in France, and every inch under cultivation. It is what the French call *une paysage riante*, and I assure you, it does more than smile these lovely

June mornings. I am up every morning almost as soon as the sun, and I slip my feet into *sabots*, wrap myself in a big cloak, and run right on to the lawn to make sure that the panorama has not disappeared in the night. There always lie— too good almost to be true—miles and miles of laughing country, little white towns just smiling in the early light, a thin strip of river here and there, dimpling and dancing, stretches of fields of all colours—all so peaceful and so gay, and so " chummy " that it gladdens the opening day, and makes me rejoice to have lived to see it. I never weary of it. It changes every hour, and I never can decide at which hour it is the loveliest. After all, it is a rather nice world.

Now get out your map and locate me. You will not find Huiry. But you can find Esbly, my nearest station on the main line of the Eastern Railroad. Then you will find a little narrow-gauge road running from there to Crécy-la-Chapelle. Halfway between you will find Couilly-Saint-Germain. Well, I am right up the hill, about a third of the way between Couilly and Meaux.

It is a nice historic country. But for that matter so is all France. I am only fifteen miles north-east of Bondy, in whose forest the naughty Queen Fredegonde, beside whose tomb, in Saint-Denis, we have often stood together, had her husband killed, and nearer still to Chelles, where the Merovingian kings once had a palace stained with the blood of many crimes, about which you read, in many awful details, in Maurice Strauss's "Tragique Histoire des Reines Brunhaut et Fredegonde," which I remember to have sent you when it first came out. Of course no trace of those days of the Merovingian dynasty remains here or anywhere else. Chelles is now one of the fortified places in the outer belt of forts surrounding Paris.

So, if you will not accept all this as an explanation of what you are pleased to call my "desertion," may I humbly and reluctantly put up a plea for my health, and hope for a sympathetic hearing?

If I am to live much longer,—and I am on the road down the hill, you know,—I demand of Life my physical well-being. I want a robust old age. I feel that I could never hope to have that much longer in town,—city-born and city-bred though I am. I used to think, and I continued to think for a long time, that I could not live if my feet did not press a city pavement. The fact that I have changed my mind seems to me, at my age, a sufficient excuse for, as frankly, changing my habits. It surely proves that I have not a sick will—yet. In the simple life I crave—digging in the earth, living out of doors —I expect to earn the strength of which city life and city habits were robbing me. I believe I can. Faith half wins a battle. No one ever dies up on this hill, I am told, except of hard

drink. Judging by my experience with workmen here, not always of that. I never saw so
many very old, very active, robust people in so
small a space in all my life as I have seen here.

Are you answered?

Yet if, after all this expenditure of words, you
still think I am shirking—well, I am sorry. It
seems to me that, from another point of view,
I am doing my duty, and giving the younger
generation more room—getting out of the lime-
light, so to speak, which, between you and me,
was getting trying for my mental complexion.
If I have blundered, the consequences be on my
own head. My hair could hardly be whiter—
that's something. Besides, retreat is not cut off.
I have sworn no eternal oath not to change my
mind again.

In any case you have no occasion to worry
about me: I've a head full of memories. I am
going to classify them, as I do my books. Some
of them I am going to forget, just as I reject
books that have ceased to interest me. I know
the latter is always a wrench. The former may
be impossible. I shall not be lonely. No one
who reads is ever that. I may miss talking.
Perhaps that is a good thing. I may have
talked too much. That does happen.

Remember one thing—I am not inaccessible.
I may now and then get an opportunity to talk
again, and in a new background. Who knows?
I am counting on nothing but the facts about

me. So come on, Future. I've my back against the past. Anyway, as you see, it is too late to argue. I've crossed the Rubicon, and can return only when I have built a new bridge.

## II

THAT'S right. Accept the situation. You
will soon find that Paris will seem the
same to you. Besides, I had really given all I
had to give there.

Indeed, you shall know, to the smallest de-
tail, just how the material side of my life is
arranged—all my comforts and discomforts—
since you ask.

I am now absolutely settled into my little
"hole" in the country, as you call it. It has
been so easy. I have been here now nearly three
weeks. Everything is in perfect order. You
would be amazed if you could see just how
everything fell into place. The furniture has
behaved itself beautifully. There are days when
I wonder if either I or it ever lived anywhere
else. The shabby old furniture with which you
were long so familiar just slipped right into place.
I had not a stick too little, and could not have
placed another piece. I call that "bull luck."

I have always told you—you have not always
agreed—that France was the easiest place in the
world to live in, and the love of a land in which
to be a pauper. That is why it suits me.

15

Don't harp on that word "alone." I know I am living alone, in a house that has four outside doors into the bargain. But you know I am not one of the "afraid" kind. I am not boasting. That is a characteristic, not a quality. One is afraid or one is not. It happens that I am not. Still, I am very prudent. You would laugh if you could see me "shutting up" for the night. All my windows on the ground floor are heavily barred. Such of the doors as have glass in them have shutters also. The window shutters are primitive affairs of solid wood, with diamond-shaped holes in the upper part. First, I put up the shutters on the door in the dining-room which leads into the garden on the south side; then I lock the door. Then I do a similar service for the kitchen door on to the front terrace, and that into the orchard, and lock both doors. Then I go out of the salon door and lock the stable and the grange and take out the keys. Then I come into the salon and lock the door after me, and push two of the biggest bolts you ever saw. After which I hang up the keys, which are as big as the historic key of the Bastille, which you may remember to have seen at the Musée Carnavalet. Then I close and bolt all the shutters downstairs. I do it systematically every night—because I promised not to be fool-hardy. I always grin, and feel as if it were a scene in a play. It impresses me so much like a tre-mendous piece of business—dramatic suspense

—which leads up to nothing except my going quietly upstairs to bed.

When it is all done I feel as I used to in my strenuous working days, when, after midnight, all the rest of the world — my little world—being calmly asleep, I cuddled down in the corner of my couch to read;—the world is mine!

Never in my life—anywhere, under any circumstances—have I been so well taken care of. I have a *femme de ménage*—a sort of cross between a housekeeper and a maid-of-all-work. She is a married woman, the wife of a farmer whose house is three minutes away from mine. My dressing-room window and my dining-room door look across a field of currant bushes to her house. I have only to blow on the dog's whistle and she can hear. Her name is Amélie, and she is a character, a nice one, but not half as much of a character as her husband—her second. She is a Parisian. Her first husband was a jockey, half Breton, half English. He died years ago when she was young: broke his neck in a big race at Auteuil.

She has had a checkered career, and lived in several smart families, before, to assure her old age, she married this gentle, queer little farmer. She is a great find for me. But the thing balances up beautifully, as I am a blessing to her, a new interest in her monotonous life, and she never lets me forget how much happier she is since I came here to live. She is very bright and gay, intelligent enough to be a companion when I need one, and well-bred enough to fall right into her proper place when I don't.

Her husband's name is Abélard. Oh, yes, of course, I asked him about Héloïse the first time I saw him, and I was staggered when the little old toothless chap giggled and said, " That was before my time." What do you think of that ? Everyone calls him " Père Abélard," and about the house it is shortened down to " Père." He is over twenty years older than Amélie—well along in his seventies. He is a native of the commune—was born at Pont-aux-Dames, at the foot of the hill, right next to the old abbaye of that name. He is a type familiar enough to those who know French provincial life. His father was a well-to-do farmer. His mother was the typical mother of her class. She kept her sons under her thumb as long as she lived. Père Abélard worked on his father's farm. He had his living, but never a sou in his pocket. The only diversion he ever had was playing the violin, which some passer in the commune taught him. When his parents died, he and his brothers sold the old place at Pont-aux-Dames to Coquelin, who was preparing to turn the historic old convent into a *maison de retraite* for aged actors, and he came up here on the hill and bought his present farm in this hamlet, where almost every one is some sort of a cousin of his.

Oddly enough, almost every one of these female cousins has a history. You would not think it, to look at the place and the people, yet I fancy that it is pretty universal for women in such places to have "histories." You will see an old woman with a bronzed face—sometimes still handsome, often the reverse—in her short skirt, her big apron tied round where a waist is not, her still beautiful hair concealed in a coloured handkerchief. You ask the question of the right person, and you will discover that she is rich; that she is avaricious; that she pays heavy taxes; denies herself all but the bare necessities; and that the foundation of her fortune dates back to an *affaire du cœur*, or perhaps of interest, possibly of cupidity; and that very often the middle-aged daughter who still "lives at home with mother," had also had a profitable *affaire* arranged by mother herself. Everything has been perfectly *convenable*. Every one either knows about it or has forgotten it. No one is bothered or thinks the worse of her so long as she has remained of the "people" and put on no airs. But let her attempt to rise out of her class, or go up to Paris, and the Lord help her if she ever wants to come back, and, French fashion, end her days where she began them. This is typically, provincially French. When you come down here I shall tell you tales that will make Balzac and De Maupassant look tame.

You have no idea how little money these

people spend. It must hurt them terribly to cough up their taxes. They all till the land, and eat what they grow. Amélie's husband spends exactly four cents a week—to get shaved on Sunday. He can't shave himself. A razor scares him to death. He looks as if he were going to the guillotine when he starts for the barber's, but she will not stand for a beard of more than a week's growth. He always stops at my door on his way back to let his wife kiss his clean old face, all wreathed with smiles—the ordeal is over for another week. He never needs a sou except for that shave. He drinks nothing but his own cider: he eats his own vegetables, his own rabbits; he never goes anywhere except to the fields,— does not want to,—unless it is to play the violin for a dance or a fête. He just works, eats, sleeps, reads his newspaper, and is content. Yet he pays taxes on nearly a hundred thousand francs' worth of real estate.

But, after all, this is not what I started to tell you—that was about my domestic arrangements. Amélie does everything for me. She comes early in the morning, builds a fire, then goes across the field for the milk while water is heating. Then she arranges my bath, gets my coffee, tidies up the house. She buys everything I need, cooks for me, waits on me, even mends for me,—all for the magnificent sum of eight dollars a month. It really isn't as much as that, it is forty francs a month, which comes to about a dollar and eighty cents a week in your currency. She has on her farm everything in the way of vegetables that I need, from potatoes to "asparagras," from peas to tomatoes. She has chickens and eggs. Bread, butter, cheese, meat, come right to the gate; so does the letter carrier, who not only brings my mail but takes it away. The only thing we have to go for is the milk.

To make it seem all the more primitive there is a rickety old diligence which runs from Quincy —Huiry is really a suburb of Quincy—to Esbly twice a day, to connect with trains for Paris with which the branch road does not connect. It has an imperial, and when you come out to see me, at some future time, you will get a lovely view of the country from a top seat. You could walk the four miles quicker than the horse does,—it is uphill nearly all the way,—but time is no longer any object with *me*. Amélie has a donkey and a little cart to drive me to the station at Couilly when I take that line, or when I want to do an errand or go to the laundress, or merely to amuse myself.

If you can really match this for a cheap, easy, simple way for an elderly person to live in dignity, I wish you would. It is far easier than living in Paris was, and living in Paris was easier for me than the States. I am sorry, but it is the truth.

You ask me what I do with the "long days." My dear! they are short, and yet I am out of bed a little after four every morning. To be sure I get into bed again at half past eight, or, at latest, nine, every night. Of course the weather is simply lovely. As soon as I have made sure that my beloved panorama has not disappeared in the night I dress in great haste. My morning toilette consists of a long black studio apron such as the French children wear to school,—it takes the place of a dress,—felt shoes inside my *sabots*, a big hat, and long gardening-gloves. In that get-up I weed a little, rake up my paths, examine my fruit trees, and, at intervals, lean on my rake in a Maud Muller posture, and gaze at the view. It is never the same two hours of the day, and I never weary of looking at it.

My garden would make you chortle with glee. You will have to take it by degrees, as I do. I have a sort of bowing acquaintance with it myself—*en masse*, so to speak. I hardly know a thing in it by name. I have wall fruit on the south side and an orchard of plum, pear, and cherry trees on the north side. The east side is half lawn and half disorderly flower beds. I am going to let the tangle in the orchard grow at its own sweet will—that is, I am going to as far as Amélie allows me. I never admire some trailing, flowering thing there but that, while I am admiring it, Amélie comes out and pulls it out of the ground, declaring it *une saleté* and will poison the whole place if allowed to grow.

Yet some of these same *saletés* are so pretty and grow so easily that I am tempted not to care. One of these trials of my life is what I am learning to know as *liserone*—we used to call it wild morning-glory. *That* I am forbidden to have—if I want anything else. But it is pretty.

I remember years ago to have heard Ysolet, in a lecture at the Sorbonne, state that the "struggle for life" among the plants was fiercer and more tragic than that among human beings. It was mere words to me then. In the short three weeks that I have been out here in my hilltop garden I have learned to know how true that was. Sometimes I am tempted to have a garden of weeds. I suppose my neighbours would object if I let them all go to seed and sow these sins of agriculture all over the tidy farms about me.

Often these lovely mornings I take a long walk with the dog before breakfast. He is an Airedale, and I am terribly proud of him and my neighbours terribly afraid of him. I am half inclined to believe that he is as afraid of them as they are of him, but I keep that suspicion, for prudential reasons, to myself. At any rate, all passers keep at a respectful distance from me and him.

Our usual walk is down the hill to the north, toward the shady route that leads by the edge of the canal to Meaux. We go along the fields,

down the long hill until we strike into a foot-
path which leads through the woods to the road
called "Pavés du Roi" and on to the canal,
from which a walk of five minutes takes us to
the Marne. After we cross the road at the foot
of the hill there is not a house, and the country
is so pretty—undulating ground, in every tint
of green and yellow. From the high bridge that
crosses the canal the picture is—well, is French-
canally, and you know what that means—green-
banked, tree-shaded, with a towpath bordering
the straight line of water, and here and there a
row of broad long canal-boats moving slowly
through the shadows.

By the time I get back I am ready for breakfast. You know I never could eat or drink
early in the morning. I have my coffee in the
orchard under a big pear tree, and I have the
inevitable book propped against the urn. Needless to say I never read a word. I simply look
at the panorama. All the same I have to have
the book there or I could not eat, just as I can't
go to sleep without books on the bed.

After breakfast I write letters. Before I know
it Amélie appears at the library door to announce
that "Madame est servie"—and the morning
is gone. As I am alone, as a rule I take my
lunch in the breakfast-room. It is on the north
side of the house, and is the coolest room in
the house at noon. Besides, it has a window
overlooking the plain. In the afternoon I read

and write and mend, and then I take a light supper in the arbour on the east side of the house under a crimson rambler, one of the first ever planted here over thirty years ago.

I must tell you about that crimson rambler. You know when I hired this house it was only a peasant's hut. In front of what is now the kitchen—it was then a dark hole for fuel—stood four dilapidated posts, moss-covered and decrepit, over which hung a tangle of something. It was what I called a "mess." I was not as educated as I am now. I saw—it was winter—what looked to me an unsightly tangle of disorder. I ordered those posts down. My workmen, who stood in some awe of me,—I was the first American they had ever seen,—were slow in obeying. They did not dispute the order, only they did not execute it.

One day I was very stern. I said to my head mason, "I have ordered that thing removed half a dozen times. Be so good as to have those posts taken down before I come out again."

He touched his cap, and said, "Very well, madame."

It happened that the next time I came out the weather had gotten spring-like. The posts were down. The tangle that had grown over them was trailing on the ground—but it had begun to put out leaves. I looked at it—and for the first time it occurred to me to say, "What *is* that?"

The mason looked at me a moment, and

replied, "That, madame! That is a 'creamson ramblaire'—the oldest one in the commune."

Poor fellow, it had never occurred to him that I did not know.

Seven feet to the north of the climbing-rose bush was a wide hedge of tall lilac bushes. So I threw up an arbour between them, and the crimson rambler now mounts eight feet in the air. It is a glory of colour to-day, and my pride. But didn't I come near to losing it?

The long evenings are wonderful. I sit out until nine, and can read until almost the last minute. I never light a lamp until I go up to bed. That is my day. It seems busy enough to me. I am afraid it will—to you, still so willing to fight, still so absorbed in the struggle, and and still so over-fond of your species—seem futile. Who knows which of us is right?—or if our difference of opinion may not be a difference in our years? If all who love one another were of the same opinion, living would be monotonous, and conversation flabby. So cheer up. You are content. Allow me to be.

# III

I HAVE just received your letter—the last, you say, that you can send before you sail away again for "The Land of the Free and the Home of the Brave," where you still seem to feel that it is my duty to return to die. I vow I will not discuss that with you again. Poverty is an unpretty thing, and poverty plus old age simply horrid in the wonderful land which saw my birth, and to which I take off my sun-bonnet in reverent admiration, in much the same spirit that the peasants still uncover before a shrine. But it is the land of the young, the energetic, and the ambitious, the ideal home of the very rich and the labouring classes. I am none of those—hence here I stay. I turn my eyes to the west often with a queer sort of amazed pride. If I were a foreigner—of any race but French—I'd work my passage out there in an emigrant ship. As it is, I did forty-five years of hard labour there, and I consider that I earned the freedom to die where I please.

I can see in " my mind's eye " the glitter in yours as you wrote—and underscored—" I'll wager you spend half your days in writing letters back to the land you have wilfully deserted. As well have stayed among us and talked—and you talk so much better than you write." Tut! tut! That is nasty. Of course I do not deny that I shall miss the inspiration of your contradictions—or do you call it repartee? I scorn your arguments, and I hereby swear that you shall not worry another remonstrance from me.

You ask me how it happens that I wandered in this direction, into a part of the country about which you do not remember ever to have heard me talk, when there were so many places that would have seemed to you to be more interesting. Well, this is more interesting than you think. You must not fancy that a place is not interesting because you can't find it in Hare, and because Henry James never talked about it. That was James's misfortune and not his fault.

The truth is I *did* look in many more familiar directions before fortunate accident led me here. I had an idea that I wanted to live on the heights of Montmorency, in the Jean Jacques Rousseau country. But it was terribly expensive—too near to Enghein and its Casino and baccarat tables. Then I came near to taking a house near Viroflay, within walking distance of Versailles. But at the very mention of that all my French friends simply howled. "It was too near to Paris"; "it was the chosen route of the

Apaches "; and so on and so forth. I did not so
much care for the situation. It was too familiar,
and it was not really country, it was only
suburbs. But the house attracted me. It was
old and quaint, and the garden was pretty, and
it was high. Still it *was* too expensive. After
that I found a house well within my means at
Poigny, about an hour, by diligence from Rambouillet. That did attract me. It was real
country, but it had no view and the house was
very small. Still I had got so tired of hunting
that I was actually on the point of taking it
when one of my friends accidentally found this
place. If it had been made to order it could not
have suited me better—situation, age, price, all
just to my taste. I put over a year and a half
into the search. Did I keep it to myself well?

Besides, the country here had a certain novelty
to me. I know the country on the other side of
the Petit Morin, but all this is new to me except
Meaux. At first the house did not look habit-
able to me. It was easily made so, however,
and it has great possibilities, which will keep me
busy for years.

Although you do not know this part of the
country, it has, for me, every sort of attraction—
historical as well as picturesque. Its historical
interest is rather for the student than the tourist,
and I love it none the less for that.

If ever you relent and come to see me, I can
take you for some lovely walks. I can, on a

Sunday afternoon, in good weather, even take you to the theatre—what is more, to the theatre to see the players of the Comédie Française. It is only half an hour's walk from my house to Pont-aux-Dames, where Coquelin set up his *maison de retraite* for aged actors, and where he died and is buried. In the old park, where the du Barry used to walk in the days when Louis XVI clapped her in prison on a warrant wrung from the dying old king, her royal lover, there is an open-air theatre, and there, on Sundays, the actors of the Théâtre Français play, within sight of the tomb of the founder of the retreat, under the very trees—and they are stately and noble— where the du Barry walked.

Of course I shall only take you there if you insist. I have outgrown the play-house. I fancy that I am much more likely to sit out on the lawn and preach to you on how the theatre has missed its mission than I am—unless you insist —to take you down to the hill to listen to Molière or Racine.

If, however, that bores you,—it would me,— you can sit under the trees and close your eyes while I give you a Stoddard lecture without the slides. I shall tell you about the little walled town of Crécy, still surrounded by its moat, where the tiny little houses stand in gardens with their backs on the moat, each with its tiny foot-bridge, that pulls up, just to remind you that it was once a royal city, with drawbridge and portcullis, a city in which kings used to stay, and in which Jeanne d'Arc slept one night on her way back from crowning *her* king at Rheims : a city that once boasted ninety-nine towers. Half a dozen of these towers still stand. Their thick walls are now pierced with windows, in which muslin curtains blow in the wind, to say that to-day they are the humble homes of simple people, and to remind you of what warfare was in the days when such towers were a defence. Why, the very garden in which you will be sitting when I tell you this was once a part of the royal estate, and the last Lord of the Land was the Duc de Penthièvre. I thought that fact rather amusing when I found it out, considering that the house I came so near to taking at Poigny was on the Rambouillet estate where his father, the Duc de Toulouse, one of Louis XIV's illegitimate sons, died, where the Duc de Penthièvre was born, and where he buried his naughty son, the Duc de Lamballe.

Of course, while I am telling you things like this you will have to bring your imagination into play, as very few vestiges of the old days remain. I still get just as much fun out of *Il y avait une fois*, even when the " once on a time " can only be conjured up with closed eyes. Still, I can show you some dear little old chapels, and while I am telling you about it you will probably hear the far-off, sad tolling of a bell, and I shall say to you " *Ça sonne à Bouleurs.*" It will be the church bells at Bouleurs, a tiny, tree-shaded hamlet, on another hilltop, from which, owing to its situation, the bells, which rarely ring save for a funeral, can be heard at a great distance, as they have rung over the valley for years. They sound so sad in the still air that the expression, *Ça sonne à Bouleurs*, has come to mean bad luck. In all the towns where the bell can be heard, a man who is having bad luck at cards, or has made a bad bargain, or has been tricked in any way invariably remarks," *Ça sonne à Bouleurs.*"

I could show you something more modern in the way of historical association. For example, from the road at the south side of my hill I can show you the Château de la Haute Maison, with its mansard and Louis XVI pavilions, where Bismarck and Favre had their first unsuccessful meeting, when this hill was occupied by the Germans in 1870 during the siege of Paris. And fifteen minutes' walk from here is the pretty Château de Condé, which was then the home of Casimir-Perier, and if you do not remember him as the President of the Republic who resigned rather than face the Dreyfus case, you may remember him as the father-in-law of Madame Simone, who unsuccessfully stormed the American theatre, two years ago.

You ask me how isolated I am. Well, I am, and I am not. My house stands in the middle of my garden. That is a certain sort of isolation.

There is a house on the opposite side of the road, much nearer than I wish it were. Luckily it is rarely occupied. Still, when it is, it is over-occupied. At the foot of the hill—perhaps five hundred yards away—are the tiny hamlet of Joncheroy and the little village of Voisins. Just above me is the hamlet of Huiry—half a dozen houses. You see that is not sad. So cheer up. So far as I know the commune has no criminal record, and I am not on the route of tramps. Remember, please, that, in those last winters in Paris, I did not prove immune to contagions. There is nothing for me to catch up here—unless it be the gaiety with which the air is saturated.

You ask me also how it happens that I am living again near by "Quincy." As true as you live, I never thought of the coincidence. If you please, we pronounce it "Kansee." When I read your question I laughed. I remembered that Abélard, when he was first condemned, re-tired to the Hermitage of Quincy, but when I took down Larousse to look it up, what do you think I found? Simply this and nothing more: "Quincy: Ville des Etats-Unis (Massachusetts), 28,000 habitants."

Isn't that droll? However, I know that there was a Sire de Quincy centuries ago, so I will look him up and let you know what I find.

The morning paper—always late here—brings the startling news of the assassination of the Crown Prince of Austria. What an unlucky family that has been! Franz Josef must be a tough old gentleman to have stood up against so many shocks. I used to feel so sorry for him when Fate dealt him another blow that would have been a " knock-out " for most people. But he has stood so many, and outlived happier people, that I begin to believe that if the wind is tempered to the shorn lamb, the hides, or the hearts, of some people are toughened to stand the gales of Fate.

Well, I imagine that Austria will not grieve much—though she may be mad—over the loss of a none too popular crown prince, whose morganatic wife could never be crowned, whose children cannot inherit, and who could only have kept the throne warm for a while for the man who now steps into line a little sooner than he would have had this not happened. If a man will be a crown prince in these times he must take the consequences. We do get hard-hearted, and no mistake, when it is not in our family that the lightning strikes. The " Paths of Glory lead but to the grave," so what matters it, really, out by what door one goes ?

This will reach you soon after you arrive in the great city of tall buildings. More will follow, and I expect they will be so gay that you will rejoice to have even a postal tie with La Belle France, to which, if you are a real good American, you will come back when you die—if you do not before.

# IV

YOUR Fourth of July letter came this morning. It was lively reading, especially coming so soon after my first *Quatorze juillet* in the country. The day was a great contrast to the many remembrances I have of Bastille Day in Paris. How I remember my first experience of that fête, when my bedroom window overlooked one of the squares where the band played for the three nights of dancing. That was a fierce experience after the novelty of the first night had worn off, when hour after hour the dance music droned on, and hour after hour the dancing feet on the pavement nearly drove me frantic. To offset it I have memories of the Champs-Elysées and the Place de l'Hôtel de Ville turned into a fairyland. I am glad I saw all that. The memory hangs in my mind like a lovely picture. Out here it was all as still as— I was going to say Sunday, but I should have to say a New England Sunday, as out here Sunday is just like any other day. There was not even a ringing of bells. The only difference there was to me was that Amélie drove Père over to Coutevroult, on the other side of the valley of the Grand Morin, where he played for the dance, and did not get back until long after daylight. I did put out my flags in honour of the day. That was the extent of my celebrating.

In the evening there was a procession at Voisins, and from Meaux and the other towns on the hill there was an occasional rocket. It was not really an exciting day.

The procession at Voisins was a primitive affair, but, to me, all the prettier for that. It looked so quaint with its queer lanterns, its few flags, its children and men in blouses, strolling through the crooked, hilly streets of the old town, to the tap of the drum. No French procession, except it be soldiers, ever marches. If you ever saw a funeral procession going through the street, or one going about a church, you do not need to be told that.

I was glad that this little procession here kept so much of its old-time character, but I was sorry it was not gayer. Still, it was so picturesque that it made me regret anew, what I have so many times regretted of late years, that so many of the old habits of country life in France are passing away, as they are, for that matter, all over Europe, along with ignorance and national costumes.

I must tell you that up to three years ago it was the custom in this commune, which, simply because it is not on a railroad, has preserved its old-days air and habits, for wedding and bap-

tismal parties to walk in procession through the
streets from the house to the church and back
again. Père Abélard used to head the procession, playing on his violin. There has been but
one event of that kind since I came, and I am
afraid it will be the last. That was for the bap-
tism of the first grandchild of a French officer
who had married a woman born in this commune, and the older members of the family had a
desire to keep up the old traditions. The church
is at Quincy, just a step off the *route nationale*
to Meaux. Père walked ahead,—he could not
be accused of marching,—fiddling away for dear
life. The pretty young godmother carried the
baby, in its wonderful christening finery, walking between the grandmother and the father,
and the guests, all in their gayest clothes, followed on as they liked behind, all stepping out
a little on account of the fiddle ahead. They
came back from the church in the same way,
only father carried the baby, and the godmother
scattered her largesse among the village children.

It is a pity that such pretty customs die out.
Wedding parties must have looked so attractive
going along these country roads. The fashion
that has replaced it is unattractive. To-day they
think it much more *chic* to hire a big barge and
drive down to Esbly and have a rousing breakfast and dance in the big hall which every
country hotel has for such festivities. Such
changes are in the spirit of the times, so I sup-

pose one must not complain. I should not if people were any happier, but I cannot see that they are. However, I suppose that will come when the Republic is older. The responsibility which that has put on the people has made them more serious than they used to be.

I don't blame you for laughing at the idea of me in a donkey cart. You would laugh harder if you could *see* the cart and me. I do look droll. But this is the land where nothing astonishes any one, thank Heaven. But you wait until I get my *complet de velours*—which is to say my velveteens. I shall match up with the rig then, never fear. Rome was not built in a day, nor can a lady from the city turn into a country-looking lady in the wink of an eye. By the time you have sufficiently overcome your prejudices as to come out and see me with your own eyes, I'll fit into the landscape and the cart in great style.

Absolutely no news to write you, unless you will consider it news that my hedge of dahlias, which I planted myself a month ago, is coming up like nothing else in the world but Jack's Beanstalk. Nothing but weeds ever grew so rank before. Père says I was too generous with my biogene—the latest French thing in fertilizers. But I did want them to be nourished in a rich soil—and come up quick. They did. I can actually see them grow. I am almost afraid to tell you that they are over two feet high now.

Of course you won't believe me. But it is not a fairy tale. I would not have believed it myself if I had not seen it.

Alas! I find that I cannot break myself of reading the newspapers, and reading them eagerly. It is all the fault of that nasty affair in Bosnia. I have a dim recollection that I was very flippant about it in my last letter to you. After all, woman proposes and politics upset her proposition. There seems to be no quick remedy for habit, more's the pity. It is a nasty outlook. We are simply holding our breaths here.

# V

THIS will be only a short letter—more to
keep my promise to you than because I
feel in the mood to write. Events have broken
that. It looks, after all, as if the Servian affair
was to become a European affair, and that, what
looked as if it might happen during the Balkan
War is really coming to pass—a general European uprising.

It is an odd thing. It seems it is an easy
thing to change one's environment, but not so
easy to change one's character. I am just as
excited over the ugly business as I should have
been had I remained near the boulevards, where
I could have got a newspaper half a dozen times
a day. I only get one a day, and this morning
I got that one with difficulty. My "Figaro,"
which comes out by mail, has not come at all.

Well, it seems that the so-called "alarmists"
were right. Germany has NOT been turning her
nation into an army just to divert her popula-
tion, nor spending her last mark on ships just
to amuse herself, and keep Prince Henry busy.

I am sitting here this morning, as I suppose
all France is doing, simply holding my breath

40

to see what England is going to do. I imagine
there is small doubt about it. I don't see how
she can do anything but fight. It is hard to
realize that a big war is inevitable, but it looks
like it. It was staved off, in spite of Germany's
perfidy, during the Balkan troubles. If it has
to come now, just imagine what it is going to
mean! It will be the bloodiest affair the world
has ever seen—a war in the air, a war under
the sea as well as on it, and carried out with the
most effective man-slaughtering machines ever
used in battle.

I need not tell you—you know, we have so
often talked about it—how I feel about war.
Yet many times since I came to France to live,
I have felt as if I could bear another one, if only
it gave Alsace and Lorraine back to us—us
meaning me and France. France really deserves
her revenge for the humiliation of 1870 and
that beastly Treaty of Frankfort. I don't deny
that 1870 was the making of modern France,
or that, since the Treaty of Frankfort, as a
nation she has learned a lesson of patience that
she sorely needed. But now that Germany is
preparing—is really prepared to attack her again
—well, the very hair on my head rises up at
the idea. There have been times in the last ten
years when I have firmly believed that she could
not be conquered again. But Germany! Well,
I don't know. If she is, it will not be for lack
of nerve or character. Still, it is no secret that

she is not ready, or that the anti-military party is strong,—and with that awful Caillaux affair I swore to myself that nothing should tempt me to speak of it. It has been so disgraceful. Still, it is so in the air just now that it has to be recognized as pitifully significant and very menacing to political unity.

The tension here is terrible. Still, the faces of the men are stern, and every one is so calm— the silence is deadly. There is an absolute suspension of work in the fields. It is as if all France was holding its breath.

One word before I forget it again. You say that you have asked me twice if I have any friend near me. I am sure I have already answered that—yes! I have a family of friends at Voulangis, about two miles the other side of Crécy-en-Brie. Of course neighbours do not see one another in the country as often as in the city, but there they are, so I hasten to relieve your mind just now, when there is a menace of war, and I am sitting tight on my hilltop on the road to the frontier.

# VI

WELL, dear, what looked impossible is evidently coming to pass.

Early yesterday morning the *garde champêtre* —who is the only thing in the way of a policeman that we have—marched up the road beating his drum. At every crossroad he stopped and read an order. I heard him at the foot of the hill, but I waited for him to pass. At the top of the hill he stopped to paste a bill on the door of the carriage-house on Père Abélard's farm. You can imagine me,—in my long studio apron, with my head tied up in a muslin cap,—running up the hill to join the group of poor women of the hamlet, to read the proclamation to the armies of land and sea—the order for the mobilization of the French military and naval forces—headed by its crossed French flags. It was the first experience in my life of a thing like that. I had a cold chill down my spine as I realized that it was not so easy as I had thought to separate myself from Life. We stood there together—a little group of women—and silently read it through—this command for the rising up of a Nation. No need for the men to read it. Each with his military papers in his pocket knew the moment he heard the drum what it meant, and knew equally well his place. I was a foreigner among them, but I forgot that, and if any of them remembered they made no sign. We did not say a word to one another. I silently returned to my garden and sat down. War again! This time war close by—not war about which one can read, as one reads it in the newspapers, as you will read it in the States, far away from it, but war right here—if the Germans can cross the frontier.

It came as a sort of shock, though I might have realized it yesterday when several of the men of the commune came to say *au revoir*, with the information that they were joining their regiments, but I felt as if some way other than cannon might be found out of the situation. War had not been declared—has not to-day. Still, things rarely go to this length and stop there. Judging by this morning's papers Germany really wants it. She could have, had she wished, held stupid Austria back from the throat of poor Servia, not yet recovered from her two Balkan wars.

I imagine this letter will turn into a sort of diary, as it is difficult to say when I shall be able to get any mail matter off. All our communications with the outside world—except by road—were cut this morning by order of the War Bureau. Our railroad is the road to all the eastern frontiers—the trains to Belgium as well as to Metz and Strasbourg pass within sight of my garden. If you don't know what that means—just look on a map and you will realize that the army that advances, whether by road or by train, will pass by me.

During the mobilization, which will take weeks,—not only is France not ready, all the world knows that her fortified towns are mostly only fortified on the map,—civilians, the mails, and such things must make way for soldiers and war materials. I shall continue to write. It will make me feel in touch still; it will be something to do: besides, any time some one may go up to town by road and I thus have a chance to send it.

# VII

WELL—war is declared.
I passed a rather restless night. I
fancy every one in France did. All night I
heard a murmur of voices, such an unusual
thing here. It simply meant that the town was
awake and, the night being warm, every one
was out of doors.

All day to-day aeroplanes have been flying
between Paris and the frontier. Everything that
flies seems to go right over my roof. Early this
morning I saw two machines meet, right over
my garden, circle about each other as if signalling, and fly off together. I could not help feeling as if one chapter of Wells's " War in the
Air " had come to pass. It did make me realize
how rapidly the aeroplane had developed into a
real weapon of war. I remember so well, no
longer ago than Exposition year,—that was
1900,—that I was standing, one day, in the old
*Galerie des Machines*, with a young engineer
from Boston. Over our heads was a huge model
of a flying machine. It had never flown, but it
was the nearest thing to success that had been
accomplished—and it expected to fly some time.

So did Darius Green, and people were still sceptical. As he looked up at it, the engineer said: "Hang it all, that dashed old thing will fly one day, but I shall probably not live to see it."

He was only thirty at that time, and it was such a few years after that it did fly, and no time at all, once it rose in the air to stay there, before it crossed the Channel. It is wonderful to think that after centuries of effort the thing flew in my time—and that I am sitting in my garden to-day, watching it sail overhead, like a bird, looking so steady and so sure. I can see them for miles as they approach and for miles after they pass. Often they disappear from view, not because they have passed a horizon line, but simply because they have passed out of the range of my vision—becoming smaller and smaller, until they seem no bigger than a tiny bird, so small that if I take my eyes off the speck in the sky I cannot find it again. It is awe-compelling to remember how these cars in the air change all military tactics. It will be almost impossible to make any big movement that may not be discovered by the opponent.

Just after breakfast my friend from Voulangis drove over in a great state of excitement, with the proposition that I should pack up and return with her. She seemed alarmed at the idea of my being alone, and seemed to think a group of us was safer. It was a point of view that had not occurred to me, and I was not able to catch it. Still, I was touched at her thoughtfulness, even though I had to say that I proposed to stay right here. When she asked me what I proposed to do if the army came retreating across my garden, I instinctively laughed. It seems so impossible this time that the Germans can pass the frontier, and get by Verdun and Toul. All the same, that other people were thinking it possible rather brought me up standing. I just looked at the little house I had arranged such a little time ago—I have only been here two months.

She had come over feeling pretty glum—my dear neighbour from Voulangis. She went away laughing. At the gate she said, "It looks less gloomy to me than it did when I came. I felt such a brave thing driving over here through a country preparing for war. I expected you to put a statue up in your garden 'To a Brave Lady.'"

I stood in the road watching her drive away, and as I turned back to the house it suddenly took on a very human sort of look. There passed through my mind a sudden realization, that, according to my habit, I had once again stuck my feet in the ground of a new home— and taken root. It is a fact. I have often looked at people who seemed to keep foot-free. I never can. If I get pulled up violently by the roots, if I have my earthly possessions pruned away, I always hurry as fast as I can, take root in a new place, and proceed to sprout a new crop of possessions which fix me there. I used, when I was younger, to envy people who could just pack a bag and move on. I am afraid that I never envied them enough to do as they did. If I had I should have done it. I find that life is pretty logical. It is like chemical action— given certain elements to begin with, contact with the fluids of Life give a certain result. After all I fancy every one does about the best he can with the gifts he has to do with. So I imagine we do what is natural to us; if we have the gift of knowing what we want and wanting it hard enough to get it. If we don't, we compromise.

I am closing this up rather hurriedly as one of the boys who joins his regiment at Fontaine-bleau will mail it in Paris as he passes through. I suppose you are glad that you got away before this came to pass.

# VIII

I HAVE your cable asking me to come "home," as you call it. Alas, my home is where my books are—they are here. Thanks all the same.

It is a week since I wrote you—and what a week. We have had a sort of intermittent communication with the outside world since the 6th, when, after a week of deprivation, we began to get letters and an occasional newspaper, brought over from Meaux by a boy on a bicycle.

After we were certain, on the 4th of August, that war was being declared all around Germany and Austria, and that England was to back France and Russia, a sort of stupor settled on us all. Day after day Amélie would run to the Mairie at Quincy to read the telegraphic bulletin —half a dozen lines of facts—that was all we knew from day to day. It is all we know now.

Day after day I sat in my garden watching the aeroplanes flying over my head, and wishing so hard that I knew what they knew. Often I would see five in the day, and one day ten. Day after day I watched the men of the commune on their way to join their *classe*. There was hardly an hour of the day that I did not

50

nod over the hedge to groups of stern, silent
men, accompanied by their women, and leading
the children by the hand, taking the short cut
to the station which leads over the hill, right by
my gate, to Couilly. It has been so thrilling
that I find myself forgetting that it is tragic. It
is so different from anything I ever saw before.
Here is a nation—which two weeks ago was
torn by political dissension—suddenly united,
and with a spirit that I have never seen before.

I am old enough to remember well the days
of our Civil War, when regiments of volunteers,
with flying flags and bands of music, marched
through our streets in Boston, on the way to
the front. Crowds of stay-at-homes, throngs of
women and children lined the sidewalks, shouting deliriously, and waving handkerchiefs, inspired by the marching soldiers, with guns on
their shoulders, and the strains of martial music,
varied with the then popular " The girl I left
behind me," or, " When this cruel war is over."
But this is quite different. There are no marching soldiers, no flying flags, no bands of music.
It is the rising up of a Nation as one man—all
classes shoulder to shoulder, with but one idea
—" Lift up your hearts, and long live France."
I rather pity those who have not seen it.

Since the day when war was declared, and
when the Chamber of Deputies—all party feeling forgotten—stood on its feet and listened to
Paul Deschanel's terse, remarkable speech, even

here in this little commune, whose silence is only broken by the rumbling of the trains passing, in view of my garden, on the way to the frontier, and the footsteps of the groups on the way to the train, I have seen sights that have moved me as nothing I have ever met in life before has done. Day after day I have watched the men and their family pass silently, and an hour later have seen the women come back leading the children. One day I went to Couilly to see if it was yet possible for me to get to Paris. I happened to be in the station when a train was going out. Nothing goes over the line yet but men joining their regiments. They were packed in like sardines. There were no uniforms—just a crowd of men —men in blouses, men in patched jackets, well-dressed men—no distinction of class; and on the platform the women and children they were leaving. There was no laughter, none of the gaiety with which one has so often reproached this race—but neither were there any tears. As the crowded train began to move, bare heads were thrust out of windows, hats were waved, and a great shout of "Vive la France" was answered by piping children's voices, and the choked voices of women—"Vive l'Armée"; and when the train was out of sight the women took the children by the hand, and quietly climbed the hill.

Ever since the 4th of August all our cross-roads have been guarded, all our railway gates closed, and also guarded—guarded by men whose only sign of being soldiers is a cap and a gun, men in blouses with a mobilization badge on their left arms, often in patched trousers and *sabots*, with stern faces and determined eyes, and one thought—" The country is in danger."

There is a crossroad just above my house, which commands the valley on either side, and leads to a little hamlet on the *route nationale* from Couilly to Meaux, and is called " La Demi-Lune "—why " Half-Moon " I don't know. It was there, on the 6th, that I saw, for the first time, an armed barricade. The gate at the railway crossing had been opened to let a cart pass, when an automobile dashed through Saint-Germain, which is on the other side of the track. The guard raised his bayonet in the air, to command the car to stop and show its papers, but it flew by him and dashed up the hill. The poor guard—it was his first experience of that sort—stood staring after the car ; but the idea that he ought to fire at it did not occur to him until it was too late. By the time it occurred to him, and he could telephone to the Demi-Lune, it had passed that guard in the same way—and disappeared. It did not pass Meaux. It simply disappeared. It is still known as the " Phantom Car." Within half an hour there was a barricade at the Demi-Lune mounted by armed men—too late, of course. However, it was not really fruitless—that barricade—as the very next day they caught three Germans there, disguised as Sisters of Charity—papers all in order—and who would have got by, after they were detected by a little boy's calling attention to their ungloved hands, if it had not been for the number of armed old men on the barricade.

What makes things especially serious here, so near the frontier, and where the military movements must be made, is the presence of so many Germans, and the bitter feeling there is against them. On the night of August 2, just when the troops were beginning to move east, an attempt was made to blow up the railroad bridge at Ile de Villenoy, between here and Meaux. The three Germans were caught with the dynamite on them—so the story goes—and are now in barracks at Meaux. But the most absolute secrecy is preserved about all such things. Not only is all France under martial law, the censorship of the press is absolute. Every one has to carry his papers, and be provided with a passport for which he is liable to be asked in simply crossing a road.

Meaux is full of Germans. The biggest department shop there is a German enterprise. Even Couilly has a German or two, and we had one in our little hamlet. But they've got to get out. Our case is rather pathetic. He was a nice chap, employed in a big fur house in Paris. He came to France when he was fifteen, has never been back, consequently has never done his military service there. Oddly enough, for some reason, he never took out his naturalization papers, so never did his service here. He has no relatives in Germany—that is to say, none with whom he has kept up any correspondence, he says. He earns a good salary, and has always been one of the most generous men in the commune, but circumstances are against him. Even though he is an intimate friend of our mayor, the commune preferred to be rid of him. He begged not to be sent back to Germany, so he went sadly enough to a concentration camp, pretty well convinced that his career here was over. Still, the French do forget easily.

Couilly had two Germans. One of them—the barber—got out quick. The other did not. But he was quietly informed by some of his neighbours—with pistols in their hands—that his room was better than his company.

The barber occupied a shop in the one principal street in the village, which is, by the way, a comparatively rich place. He had a front shop, which was a café, with a well-fitted-up bar. The back, with a well-dressed window on the street, full of toilette articles, was the barber and hairdressing-room, very neatly arranged, with modern set bowls and mirrors, cabinets full of towels, well-filled shelves of all the things that make such a place profitable. You should see it now. Its broken windows and doors stand open to the weather. The entire interior has been " efficiently " wrecked. It is as systematic a work of destruction as I have ever seen. Not a thing was stolen, but not an article was spared. All the bottles full of things to drink and all the glasses to drink out of are smashed, so are counters, tables, chairs, and shelving. In the barber shop there is a litter of broken porcelain, broken combs, and smashed-up chairs and boxes among a wreck of hair dyes, perfumes, *brillantine*, and torn towels, and an odour of *apéritifs* and cologne over it all.

Every one pretends not to know when it happened. They say, " it was found like that one morning." Every one goes to look at it—no one enters, no one touches anything. They simply say with a smile of scorn, " Good—and so well done."

There are so many things that I wish you could see. They would give you such a new point of view regarding this race—traditionally so gay, so indifferent to many things that you consider moral, so fond of their individual comfort and personal pleasure, and often so rebellious to discipline. You would be surprised— surprised at their unity, surprised at their seriousness, and often touched by their philosophical acceptance of it all.

Amélie has a stepson and daughter. The boy —named Marius—like his father plays the violin. Like many humble musicians his music is his life and he adds handsomely to his salary as a clerk by playing at dances and little concerts, and by giving lessons in the evening. Like his father he is very timid. But he accepted the war without a word, though nothing is more foreign to his nature. It brought it home to me—this rising up of a Nation in self-defence. It is not the marching into battle of an army that has chosen soldiering. It is the marching out of all the people—of every temperament—the rich, the poor, the timid and the bold, the sensitive and the hardened, the ignorant and the scholar—all men, because they happen to be males, called on not only to cry, " Vive la France," but to see to it that she does live if dying for her can keep her alive. It is a compelling idea, isn't it?

Amélie's stepdaughter is married to a big burly chap by the name of Georges Godot. He is a thick-necked, red-faced man—in the dynamite corps on the railroad, the construction department. He is used to hardships. War is as good as anything else to him. When he came to say " good-bye " he said, " Well, if I ever have the luck to come back—so much the better. If I don't, that will be all right. You can put a placque down below in the cemetery with ' Godot, Georges: Died for the country' ; and when my boys grow up they can say to their comrades, ' Papa, you know, he died on the battlefield.' It will be a sort of distinction I am not likely to earn for them any other way"; and off he went. Rather fine for a man of that class.

Even the women make no cry. As for the children—even when you would think that they were old enough to understand the meaning of these partings they make no sign, though they seem to understand all the rest of it well enough. There isn't a boy of eight in our commune who cannot tell you how it all came about, and who is not just now full of stories of 1870, which he has heard from grandma and grandpa, for, as is natural, every one talks of 1870 now. I have lived among these people, loved them and believed in them, even when their politics annoyed me, but I confess that they have given me a surprise.

# IX

I HAVE Belgium on my soul. Brave little
country that has given new proof of its
courage and nobility, and surprised the world
with a ruler who is a man, as well as king. It
occurs to me more than ever to-day in what a
wonderful epoch we have lived. I simply can't
talk about it. The suspense is so great. I heard
this morning from an officer that the English
troops are landing, though he tells me that in
London they don't yet know that the Expedition has started. If that is true, it is wonderful.
Not a word in the papers yet, but your press is
not censored as ours is. I fancy you know these
things in New York before we do, although we
are now getting a newspaper from Meaux regularly. But there is never anything illuminating
in it. The attitude of the world to the Belgian
question is a shock to me. I confess to have
expected more active indignation at such an out-
rage.

Everything is very quiet here. Our litttle
commune sent two hundred men only, but to
take two hundred able-bodied men away makes
a big hole, and upsets life in many ways. For

some days we were without bread : bakers gone. But the women took hold and, though the bread is not yet very good, it serves and will as long as flour holds out. No one complains, though we already lack many things. No merchandize can come out yet on the railroads, all the automobiles and most of the horses are gone, and shops are shy of staple things.

Really I don't know which are the more remarkable, the men or the women. You may have read the proclamation of the Minister of Agriculture to the women of France, calling on them to go into the fields and get in the crops and prepare the ground for the sowing of the winter wheat that the men on returning might not find their fields neglected nor their crops lost. You should have seen the old men and the women and the youngsters respond. It is harvest-time, you know, just as it was in the invasion of 1870.

In a few weeks it will be time to gather the fruit. Even now it is time to pick the black-currants, all of which go to England to make the jams and jellies without which no English breakfast table is complete.

For days now the women and children have been climbing the hill at six in the morning, with big hats on their heads, deep baskets on their backs, low stools in their hands. There is a big field of black-currant bushes beside my garden to the south. All day, in the heat, they sit under the bushes picking away. At sundown they carry their heavy baskets to the weighing-machine on the roadside at the foot of the hill, and stand in line to be weighed in and paid by the English buyers for Crosse and Blackwell, Beach, and such houses, who have, I suppose, some special means of transportation.

That work is, however, the regular work for the women and children. Getting in the grain is not. Yet if you could see them take hold of it you would love them. The old men do double work. Amélie's husband is over seventy. His own work in his fields and orchard would seem too much for him. Yet he and Amélie and the donkey are in the field by three o'clock every morning, and by nine o'clock he is marching down the hill, with his rake and hoe on his shoulder to help his neighbours.

There is many a woman working in the fields to-day who was not trained to it. I have a neighbour, a rich peasant, whose two sons are at the front. Her only daughter married an officer in the Engineer Corps. When her husband joined his regiment she came home to her mother with her little boy. I see her every day, in a short skirt and a big hat, leading her boy by the hand, going to the fields to help her mother. If you don't think that is fine, I do. It is only one of many cases right under my eyes.

There are old men here who thought that

their days of hard work were over, who are in
the fields working like boys.  There is our
blacksmith—old Père Marie—lame with rheu-
matism, with his white-haired wife working in
the fields from sunrise to sunset.  He cheerfully
limps up the hill in his big felt slippers, his wife
carrying the lunch basket, and a tiny black-and-
tan English dog called "Missy," who is the
family baby, and knows lots of tricks, trotting
behind, "because," as he says, "she is so much
company."  The old blacksmith is a veteran of
1870, and was for a long time a prisoner at
Königsberg.  He likes nothing better than to
rest a bit on a big stone at my gate and talk of
1870.  Like all Frenchmen of his type he is
wonderfully intelligent, full of humour, and an
omnivorous reader.  Almost every day he has a
bit of old newspaper in his pocket out of which
he reads to *la dame Américaine* as he calls me,
not being able to pronounce my name.  It is
usually something illuminating about the Germans, when it is not something prophetic.  It is
wonderful how these old chaps take it all to
heart.

All the time my heart is out there in the
north-east.  It is not my country nor my war—
yet I feel as if it were both.  All my French
friends are there, all my neighbours, and any
number of English friends will soon be, among
them the brother of the sculptor you met at
my house last winter and liked so much.  He is

with the Royal Field Artillery. His case is rather odd. He came back to England in the spring, after six years in the civil service, to join the army. His leave just expired in time for him to re-enter the army and see his first active service in this war. Fortunately men seem to take it all as a matter of course. That consoles some, I find.

I have just heard that there are two trains a day on which civilians can go up to Paris IF THERE ARE PLACES LEFT after the army is accommodated. There is no guarantee that I can get back the same day. Still, I am going to risk it. I am afraid to be any longer without money, though goodness knows what I can do with it. Besides, I find that all my friends are flying, and I feel as if I should like to say "good-bye" —I don't know why, but I feel like indulging the impulse. Anyway, I am going to try it. I am going armed with every sort of paper—provisional passport from our consul, *permis de séjour* from my mayor here, and a local permit to enter and leave Paris, which does not allow me to stay inside the fortifications after six o'clock at night, unless I get myself identified at the préfecture of the arrondissement in which I propose to stay and have my passport viséd.

## X

I SEEM to be able to get my letters off to you much more regularly than I dared to hope.

I went up to Paris on the 19th, and had to stay over one night. The trip up was long and tedious, but interesting. There were soldiers everywhere. It amused me almost to tears to see the guards all along the line. We hear so much of the wonderful equipment of the German army. Germany has been spending fortunes for years on its equipment. French taxpayers have kicked for years against spending public moneys on war preparations. The guards all along the railroad were not a jot better got up than those in our little commune. There they stand all along the track in their patched trousers and blouses and *sabots*, with a band round the left arm, a broken soldier cap, and a gun on the shoulder. Luckily the uniform and shaved head do not make the soldier.

Just before we reached Chelles we saw the first signs of actual war preparations, as there we ran inside the wire entanglements that protect the approach to the outer fortifications at Paris, and at Pantin we saw the first concentration of trains—miles and miles of made-up trains all carrying the Red Cross on their doors, and line after line of trucks with gray ammunition wagons, and cannons. We were being constantly held up to let trainloads of soldiers and horses pass. In the station we saw a long train being made up of men going to some point on the line to join their regiments. It was a crowd of men who looked the lower labouring class. They were in their working clothes, many of them almost in rags, each carrying in a bundle, or a twine bag, his few belongings, and some of them with a loaf of bread under the arm. It looked as little martial as possible but for the stern look in the eyes of even the commonest of them. I waited on the platform to see the train pull out. There was no one to see these men off. They all seemed to realize. I hope they did. I remembered the remark of the woman regarding her husband when she saw him go: " After all, I am only his wife. France is his mother "; and I hoped these poor men, to whom Fate seemed not to have been very kind, had at least that thought in the back of their minds.

I found Paris quiet, and everyone calm—that is to say, everyone but the foreigners, struggling like people in a panic to escape. In spite of the sad news—Brussels occupied Thursday, Namur fallen Monday—there is no sign of discouragement, and no sign of defeat. If it were not for the excitement around the steamship offices the city would be almost as still as death. But all the foreigners, caught here by the unexpectedness of the war, seemed to be fighting to get off by the same train and the same day to catch the first ship, and they seemed to have little realization that, first of all, France must move her troops and war material. I heard it said—it may not be true—that some of the consular officers were to blame for this, and that there was a rumour abroad among foreigners that Paris was sure to be invested, and that foreigners had been advised to get out, so that there should be as few people inside the fortifications as possible. This rumour, however, was only prevalent among foreigners. No French people that I saw seemed to have any such feeling.

Apart from the excitement which prevailed in the vicinity of the steamship offices and banks the city had a deserted look. The Paris that you knew exists no longer. Compared with it this Paris is a dead city. Almost every shop is closed, and must be until the great number of men gone to the front can be replaced in some way. There are streets in which every closed front bears, under a paper flag pasted on shutter or door, a sign saying, "Closed on account of the mobilization"; or, "All the men with the colours."

There are almost no men in the streets. There are no buses or tramways, and cabs and automobiles are rare. Some branches of the underground are running at certain hours, and the irregular service must continue until women, and men unfit for military service, replace the men so suddenly called to the flag, and that will take time, especially as so many of the organizers as well as conductors and engineers have gone. It is the same with the big shops. However, that is not important. No one is in the humour to buy anything except food.

It took me a long time to get about. I had to walk everywhere and my friends live a long way apart, and I am a miserable walker. I found it impossible to get back that night, so I took refuge with one of my friends who is sailing on Saturday. Everyone seems to be sailing on that day, and most of them don't seem to care much how they get away—"ameliorated steerage," as they call it, seems to be the fate of many of them. I can assure you that I was glad enough to get back the next day. Silent as it is here, it is no more so than Paris, and not nearly so sad, for the change is not so great. Paris is no longer our Paris, lovely as it still is.

I do not feel in the mood to do much. I work in my garden intermittently, and the harvest bug (*bête rouge* we call him here) gets in his work unintermittently on me. If things were normal this introduction to the *bête rouge* would have seemed to me a tragedy. As it is, it is unpleasantly unimportant. I clean house intermittently ; read intermittently ; write letters intermittently. That reminds me, do read Léon Daudet's "Fantômes et Vivantes"—the first volumes of his memoirs. He is a terrible example of "*Le fils à papa.*" I don't know why it is that a vicious writer, absolutely lacking in reverence, can hold one's attention so much better than a kindly one can. In this book Daudet simply smashes idols, tears down illusions, dances gleefully on sacred traditions, and I lay awake half the night reading him,—and forgot the advancing Germans. The book comes down only to 1880, so most of the men he writes about are dead, and most of them, like Victor Hugo, for example, come off very sadly.

Well, I am reconciled to living a long time now,—much longer than I wanted to before this awful thing came to pass,—just to see all the mighty good that will result from the struggle. I am convinced, no matter what happens, of the final result. I am sure even now, when the Germans have actually crossed the frontier, that France will not be crushed this time, even if she be beaten down to Bordeaux, with her back against the Bay of Biscay. Besides, did you ever know the English bulldog to let go? But it is the horror of such a war in our times that bears so heavily on my soul. After all, " civilization " is a word we have invented, and its meaning is hardly more than relative, just as is the word " religion."

# A HILLTOP ON THE MARNE

There are problems in the events that the logical spirit finds it hard to face. In every Protestant church the laws of Moses are printed on tablets on either side of the pulpit. On those laws our civil code is founded. "Thou shalt not kill," says the law. For thousands of years the law has punished the individual who settled his private quarrels with his fist or any more effective weapon, and reserved to itself the right to exact "an eye for an eye and a tooth for a tooth." And here we are to-day, in the twentieth century, when intelligent people have long been striving after a spiritual explanation of the meaning of life, trying to prove its upward trend, trying to beat out of it materialism, endeavouring to find in altruism a road to happiness, and governments can still find no better way to settle their disputes than wholesale slaughter, and that with weapons no so-called civilized man should ever have invented nor any so-called civilized government ever permitted to be made. The theory that the death penalty was a preventive of murder has long ago been exploded. The theory that by making war horrible, war could be prevented, is being exploded to-day.

And yet—I KNOW that if the thought be taken out of life that it is worth while to die for an idea a great factor in the making of national spirit will be gone. I KNOW that a long peace makes for weakness in a race. I KNOW that without war there is still death. To me this

last fact is the consolation. It is finer to die
voluntarily for an idea deliberately faced, than
to die of old age in one's bed, and the grief of
parting no one ever born can escape. Still it is
puzzling to us simple folk—the feeling that
fundamental things do not change : that the
balance of good and evil has not changed. We
change our fashions, we change our habits, we
discover now and then another of the secrets
Nature has hidden, that delving man may be
kept busy and interested. We pride ourselves
that science at least has progressed, that we are
cleaner than our progenitors. Yet we are no
cleaner than the Greeks and Romans in the
days when Athens and Rome ruled in the world,
nor do we know in what cycle all we know to-
day was known and lost. Oh, I can hear you
claiming more happiness for the masses! I
wonder. There is no actual buying and selling
in open slave markets, it is true, but the men
who built the Pyramids and dragged the stone
for Hadrian's Villa, were they any worse off
really than the workers in the mines to-day?
Upon my soul, I don't know. Life is only a
span between the Unknown and the Unknow-
able. Living is made up in all centuries of just
so many emotions. We have never, so far as I
know, invented any new one. It *is* too bad to
throw these things at you on paper which can't
answer back as you would, and right sharply I
know.

Nothing going on here except the passing now and then of a long line of Paris street buses on the way to the front. They are all mobilized and going as heroically to the front as if they were human, and going to get smashed up just the same. It does give me a queer sensation to see them climbing this hill. The little Montmartre-Saint-Pierre bus, that climbs up the hill to the funicular in front of Sacré Cœur, came up the hill bravely. It was built to climb a hill. But the Bastille-Madeleine and the Ternes-Fille de Calvaine, and Saint-Sulpice-Villette just groaned and panted and had to have their traction changed every few steps. I thought they would never get up, but they did.

Another day it was the automobile delivery wagons of the Louvre, the Bon Marché, the Printemps, Petit-Saint-Thomas, La Belle Jardinière, Potin—all the automobiles with which you are so familiar in the streets of Paris. Of course those are much lighter, and came up bravely. As a rule they are all loaded. It is as easy to take men to the front, and material that way as by railroad, since the cars go. Only once have I seen any attempt at pleasantry on these occasions. One procession went out the other day with all sorts of funny inscriptions, some not at all pretty, many blackguarding the Kaiser, and of course one with the inevitable " *A Berlin*," the first battle-cry of 1870. This time there has been very little of that. I confess

it gave me a kind of shiver to see " *A Berlin
—pour notre plaisir* " all over the bus. " On
to Berlin! " I don't see that that can be hoped
for unless the Germans are beaten to a finish on
the Rhine and the allied armies cross Germany
as conquerors, unopposed. If they only could!
It would only be what is due to Belgium that
King Albert should lead the procession "Under
the Lindens." But I doubt if the maddest war
optimist hopes for anything so well deserved as
that. I don't dare to, sure as I am of seeing
Germany beaten to her knees before the war is
closed.

## XI

OH, the things I have seen and felt since I last wrote to you over two weeks ago. Here I am again cut off from the world, and have been since the first of the month. For a week now I have known nothing of what was going on in the world outside the limits of my own vision. For that matter, since the Germans crossed the frontier our news of the war has been meagre. We got the calm, constant re-iteration—"Left wing—held by the English—forced to retreat a little." All the same, the general impression was, that in spite of that, "all was well." I suppose it was wise.

On Sunday week,—that was August 30,—Amélie walked to Esbly, and came back with the news that they were rushing trains full of wounded soldiers and Belgian *réfugiés* through toward Paris, and that the ambulance there was quite insufficient for the work it had to do. So Monday and Tuesday we drove down in the donkey cart to carry bread and fruit, water and cigarettes, and to "lend a hand."

It was a pretty terrible sight. There were long trains of wounded soldiers. There was

73

train after train crowded with Belgians—well-dressed women and children (evidently all in their Sunday best)—packed on to open trucks, sitting on straw, in the burning sun, without shelter, covered with dust, hungry and thirsty. The sight set me to doing some hard thinking after I got home that first night. But it was not until Tuesday afternoon that I got my first hint of the truth. That afternoon, while I was standing on the platform, I heard a drum beat in the street, and sent Amélie out to see what was going on. She came back at once to say that it was the *garde champêtre* calling on the inhabitants to carry all their guns, revolvers, etc., to the *mairie* before sundown. That meant the disarming of our *département*, and it flashed through my mind that the Germans must be nearer than the official announcements had told us.

While I stood reflecting a moment,—it looked serious,—I saw approaching from the west side of the track a procession of wagons. Amélie ran down the track to the crossing to see what it meant, and came back at once to tell me that they were evacuating the towns to the north of us.

I handed the basket of fruit I was holding into a coach of the train just pulling into the station, and threw my last package of cigarettes after it; and, without a word, Amélie and I went out into the street, untied the donkey, climbed into the wagon, and started for home.

By the time we got to the road which leads east to Montry, whence there is a road over the hill to the south, it was full of the flying crowd. It was a sad sight. The procession led in both directions as far as we could see. There were huge wagons of grain; there were herds of cattle, flocks of sheep; there were wagons full of household effects, with often as many as twenty people sitting aloft; there were carriages; there were automobiles with the occupants crowded in among bundles done up in sheets; there were women pushing overloaded hand-carts; there were women pushing baby-carriages; there were dogs and cats, and goats; there was every sort of a vehicle you ever saw, drawn by every sort of beast that can draw, from dogs to oxen, from boys to donkeys. Here and there was a man on horseback, riding along the line, trying to keep it moving in order and to encourage the weary. Every one was calm and silent. There was no talking, no complaining.

The whole road was, however, blocked, and, even had our donkey wished to pass,—which she did not,—we could not. We simply fell into the procession, as soon as we found a place. Amélie and I did not say a word to each other until we reached the road that turns off to the Château de Condé; but I did speak to a man on horseback, who proved to be the intendant of one of the châteaux at Daumartin, and with another who was the mayor. I simply asked from where these people had come, and was told that they were evacuating Daumartin and all the towns on the plain between there and Meaux, which meant that Monthyon, Neufmortier, Penchard, Chauconin, Barcy, Chambry, —in fact all the villages visible from my garden were being evacuated by order of the military powers.

One of the most disquieting things about this was to see the effect of the procession as it passed along the road. All the way from Esbly to Montry people began to pack at once, and the speed with which they fell into the procession was disconcerting.

When we finally escaped from the crowd into the poplar-shaded avenue which leads to the Château de Condé, I turned to look at Amélie for the first time. I had had time to get a good hold of myself.

"Well, Amélie?" I said.

"Oh, madame," she replied, "I shall stay."

"And so shall I," I answered; but I added, "I think I must make an effort to get to Paris to-morrow, and I think you had better come with me. I shall not go, of course, unless I am sure of being able to get back. We may as well face the truth: if this means that Paris is in danger, or even if it means that we may in our turn be forced to move on, I must get some money so as to be ready."

"Very well, madame," she replied as cheerfully as if the rumble of the procession behind us were not still in our ears.

The next morning—that was September 2— I woke just before daylight. There was a continual rumble in the air. At first I thought it was the passing of more *réfugiés* on the road. I threw open my blinds, and then realized that the noise was in the other direction—from the *route nationale*. I listened. I said to myself, " If that is not artillery, then I never heard any."

Sure enough, when Amélie came to get breakfast, she announced the English soldiers were at the Demi-Lune. The infantry was camped there, and the artillery had descended to Couilly and was mounting the hill on the other side of of the Morin—between us and Paris.

I said a sort of " Hm," and told her to ask Père to harness at once. As we had no idea of the hours of the trains, or even if there were any, it was best to get to Esbly as early as possible. It was nine o'clock when we arrived, to find that there should be a train at half past. The station was full. I hunted up the *chef de gare*, and asked him if I could be sure of being able to return if I went up to Paris.

He looked at me in perfect amazement.

" You want to come back ? " he asked.

" Sure," I replied.

" You can," he answered, " if you take a train about four o'clock. That may be the last."

I very nearly said, " Jiminy-cricket ! "

The train ran into the station on time, but you never saw such a sight. It was packed as the Brookline street cars used to be on the days of a baseball game. Men were absolutely hanging on the roof; women were packed on the steps that led up to the imperials to the third-class coaches. It was a perilous-looking sight. I opened a dozen coaches—all packed, standing room as well as seats, which is ordinarily against the law. I was about to give it up when a man said to me, "Madame, there are some coaches at the rear that look as if they were empty."

I make a dash down the long platform, yanked open a door, and was about to ask if I might get in, when I saw that the coach was full of wounded soldiers in khaki, lying about on the floor as well as the seats. I was so shocked that if the station master, who had run after me, had not caught me I should had fallen backward.

"Sh! madame," he whispered, "I'll find you a place"; and in another moment I found myself, with Amélie, in a compartment where there were already eight women, a young man, two children, and heaps of hand-luggage— bundles in sheets, twine bags just bulging, paper parcels, and valises. Almost as soon as we were in, the train pulled slowly out of the station.

I learned from the women that Meaux was

being evacuated. No one was remaining but the soldiers in the barracks and the archbishop. They had been ordered out by the army the night before, and the railroad was taking them free. They were escaping with what they could carry in bundles, as they could take no baggage. Their calm was remarkable—not a complaint from any one. They were of all classes, but the barriers were down.

The young man had come from farther up the line—a newspaper chap, who had given me his seat, and was sitting on a bundle. I asked him if he knew where the Germans were, and he replied that on this wing they were at Compiègne, that the centre was advancing on Coulommier, but he did not know where the Crown Prince's division was.

I was glad I had made the effort to get to town, for this began to look as if they might succeed in arriving before the circle of steel that surrounds Paris, and God knows what good that seventy-five miles of fortifications will be against the long-range cannon that battered down Liège. I had only one wish—to get back to my hut on the hill; I did not seem to want anything else.

Just before the train ran into Lagny—our first stop—I was surprised to see British soldiers washing their horses in the river, so I was not surprised to find the station full of men in khaki. They were sleeping on the benches along the wall, and standing about in groups. As to many of the French on the train this was their first sight of the men in khaki, and as there were Scotch there in their kilts, there was a good deal of excitement.

The train made a long stop in the effort to put more people into the already overcrowded coaches. I leaned forward, wishing to get some news, and the funny thing was that I could not think how to speak to those boys in English. You may think that an affectation. It wasn't. Finally, I desperately sang out:

"Hulloa, boys."

You should have seen them dash for the window. I suppose that their native tongue sounded good to them so far from home.

"Where did you come from?" I asked.

"From up yonder—a place called La Fère," one of them replied.

"What regiment?" I asked.

"Anyone else here speak English?" he questioned, running his eyes along the faces thrust out of the windows.

I told him no one did.

"Well," he said, "we are all that is left of the North Irish Horse and a regiment of Scottish Borderers."

"What are you doing here?"

"Retreating—and waiting for orders. How far are we from Paris?"

I told him about seventeen miles. He sighed,

and remarked that he thought they were nearer, and as the train started I had the idea in the back of my head that these boys actually expected to retreat inside the fortifications. *La! la!*

Instead of the half-hour the train usually takes to get up from here to Paris, we were two hours.

I found Paris much more normal than when I was there two weeks ago, though still quite unlike itself; every one perfectly calm and no one with the slightest suspicion that the battle line was so near—hardly more than ten miles beyond the outer forts. I transacted my business quickly—saw only one person, which was wiser than I knew then, and caught the four o'clock train back—we were almost the only passengers.

I had told Père not to come after us—it was so uncertain when we could get back, and I had always been able to get a carriage at the hotel in Esbly.

We reached Esbly at about six o'clock to find the stream of emigrants still passing, although the roads were not so crowded as they had been the previous day. I ran over to the hotel to order the carriage—to be told that Esbly was evacuated, the ambulance had gone, all the horses had been sold that afternoon to people who were flying. There I was faced with a walk of five miles—lame and tired. Just as I had made up my mind that what had to be done could be done,—die or no die,—Amélie came running across the street to say:

"Did you ever see such luck? Here is the old cart horse of Cousine Georges and the wagon!"

Cousine Georges had fled, it seems, since we left, and her horse had been left at Esbly to fetch the schoolmistress and her husband. So we all climbed in. The schoolmistress and her husband did not go far, however. We discovered before we had got out of Esbly that Couilly had been evacuated during the day, and that a great many people had left Voisins; that the civil government had gone to Coutevroult; that the Croix Rouge had gone. So the schoolmistress and her husband, to whom all this was amazing news, climbed out of the wagon, and made a dash back to the station to attempt to get back to Paris. I do hope they succeeded.

Amélie and I dismissed the man who had driven the wagon down, and jogged on by ourselves. I sat on a board in the back of the covered cart, only too glad for any sort of locomotion which was not "shanks's mare."

Just after we left Esbly I saw first an English officer, standing in his stirrups and signalling across a field, where I discovered a detachment of English artillery going toward the hill. A little farther along the road we met a couple of English officers—pipes in their mouths and sticks in their hands—strolling along as quietly and smilingly as if there were no such thing as war. Naturally I wished to speak to them. I was so shut in that I could see only directly in front of me, and if you ever rode behind a big cart horse I need not tell you that although he walks slowly and heavily he walks steadily, and will not stop for any pulling on the reins unless he jolly well chooses. As we approached the officers, I leaned forward and said, "Beg your pardon," but by the time they realized that they had been addressed in English we had passed. I yanked at the flap at the back of the cart, got it open a bit, looked out to find them standing in the middle of the road, staring after us in amazement.

The only thing I had the sense to call out was:

"Where d'you come from?"

One of them made an emphatic gesture with his stick, over his shoulder in the direction from which they had come.

"Where are you going?" I called.

He made the same gesture toward Esbly, and then we all laughed heartily, and by that time we were too far apart to continue the interesting conversation, and that was all the enlightenment I got out of that meeting. The sight of them and their cannon made me feel a bit serious. I thought to myself: "If the Germans are not expected here—well, it looks like it." We

# A HILLTOP ON THE MARNE

finished the journey in silence, and I was so tired when I got back to the house that I fell into bed, and only drank a glass of milk that Amélie insisted on pouring down my throat.

# XII

*September* 5, 1914.

YOU can get some idea of how exhausted I
was on that night of Wednesday, September 2, when I tell you that I waked the next
morning to find that I had a picket at my gate.
I did not know until Amélie came to get my
coffee ready the next morning—that was Thursday, September 3—can it be that it is only three
days ago! She also brought me news that they were
preparing to blow up the bridges on the Marne;
that the post-office had gone; that the English
were cutting the telegraph wires.

While I was taking my coffee, quietly, as if it
were an everyday occurrence, she said: " Well,
madame, I imagine that we are going to see the
Germans. Père is breaking an opening into the
underground passage under the stable, and we
are going to put all we can out of sight. Will
you please gather up what you wish to save, and
it can be hidden there?"

I don't know that I ever told you that all the
hill is honeycombed with those old subterranean
passages, like the one we saw at Provins. They
say that they go as far as Crécy-en-Brie, and
used to connect the royal palace there with one
on this hill.

Naturally I gave a decided refusal to any move of that sort, so far as I was concerned. My books and portraits are the only things I should be eternally hurt to survive. To her argument that the books could be put there,—there was room enough,—I refused to listen. I had no idea of putting my books underground to be mildewed. Besides, if it had been possible I would not have attempted it—and it distinctly was impossible. I felt a good deal like the Belgian *réfugiés* I had seen,—all so well dressed; if my house was going up, it was going up in its best clothes. I had just been uprooted once—a horrid operation—and I did not propose to do it again so soon. To that my mind was made up.

Luckily for me—for Amélie was as set as I was—the argument was cut short by a knock at the front door. I opened it to find standing there a pretty French girl whom I had been seeing every day, as, morning and evening, she passed my gate to and from the railway station. Sooner or later I should have told you about her if all this excitement had not put it out of my mind and my letters. I did not know her name. I had never got to asking Amélie who she was, though I was a bit surprised to find any one of her type here where I had supposed there were only farmers and peasants.

She apologized for presenting herself so informally: said she had come, " *de la parte de mama*," to ask me what I proposed to do. I replied at once, "I am staying."

She looked a little surprised: said her mother wished to do the same, but that her only brother was with the colours; that he had confided his young wife and two babies to her, and that the Germans were so brutal to children that she did not dare risk it.

"Of course, you know," she added, "that every one has left Couilly; all the shops are closed, and nearly every one has gone from Voisins and Quincy. The mayor's wife left last night. Before going she came to us and advised us to escape at once, and even found us a horse and cart—the trains are not running. So mother thought that, as you were a foreigner, and all alone, we ought not to go without at least offering you a place in the wagon—the chance to go with us."

I was really touched, and told her so, but explained that I should stay. She was rather insistent—said her mother would be so distressed at leaving me alone with only a little group of women and children about me, who might, at the last moment, be panic-stricken.

I explained to her as well as I could that I was alone in the world, poor myself, and that I could not see myself leaving all that I valued,—my home; to have which I had made a supreme effort, and for which I had already a deep affection,— to join the band of *réfugiés*, shelterless, on the road, or to look for safety in a city, which, if the Germans passed here, was likely to be besieged and bombarded. I finally convinced her that my mind was made up. I had decided to keep my face turned toward Fate rather than run away from it. To me it seemed the only way to escape a panic—a thing of which I have always had a horror.

Seeing that nothing could make me change my mind, we shook hands, wished each other luck, and, as she turned away, she said, in her pretty French: "I am sorry it is disaster that brought us together, but I hope to know you better when days are happier"; and she went down the hill.

When I returned to the dining-room I found that, in spite of my orders, Amélie was busy putting my few pieces of silver, and such bits of china from the buffet as seemed to her valuable,—her ideas and mine on that point do not jibe,—into the waste-paper baskets to be hidden underground.

I was too tired to argue. While I stood watching her there was a tremendous explosion. I rushed into the garden. The picket, his gun on his shoulder, was at the gate.

"What was that?" I called out to him.

"Bridge," he replied. "The English divisions are destroying the bridges on the Marne behind them as they cross. That means that another division is over."

I asked him which bridge it was, but of

course he did not know. While I was standing there, trying to locate it by the smoke, an English officer, who looked of middle age, tall, clean-cut, rode down the road on a chestnut horse, as slight, as clean-cut, and well groomed as himself. He rose in his stirrups to look off at the plain before he saw me. Then he looked at me, then up at the flags flying over the gate,—saw the Stars and Stripes,—smiled, and dismounted.

"American, I see," he said.

I told him I was.

"Live here?" said he.

I told him that I did.

"Staying on?" he asked.

I answered that it looked like it.

He looked me over a moment before he said, "Please invite me into your garden and show me that view."

I was delighted. I opened the gate, and he strolled in and sauntered with a long, slow stride —a long-legged stride—out on to the lawn and right down to the hedge, and looked off.

"Beautiful," he said, as he took out his field-glass, and turned up the map case which hung at his side. "What town is that?" he asked, pointing to the foreground.

I told him that it was Mareuil-on-the-Marne.

"How far off is it?" he questioned.

I told him that it was about two miles, and Meaux was about the same distance beyond it.

"What town is that?" he asked, pointing to the hill.

I explained that the town on the horizon was Penchard—not really a town, only a village; and lower down, between Penchard and Meaux, were Neufmortier and Chauconin.

All this time he was studying his map.

"Thank you. I have it," he said. "It is a lovely country, and this is a wonderful view of it, the best I have had."

For a few minutes he stood studying it in silence—alternately looking at his map and then through his glass. Then he dropped his map, put his glasses into the case, and turned to me—and smiled. He had a winning smile, sad and yet consoling, which lighted up a bronzed face, stern and weary. It was the sort of smile to which everything was permitted.

"Married?" he said.

You can imagine what he was like when I tell you that I answered right up, and only thought it was funny hours after—or at least I shook my head cheerfully.

"You don't live here alone?" he asked.

"But I do," I replied.

He looked at me bravely a moment, then off at the plain.

"Lived here long?" he questioned.

I told him that I had lived in this house only three months, but that I had lived in France for sixteen years.

Without a word he turned back toward the house, and for half a minute, for the first time in my life, I had a sensation that it looked strange for me to be an exile in a country that was not mine, and with no ties. For a penny I would have told him the history of my life. Luckily he did not give me time. He just strode down to the gate, and by the time he had his foot in the stirrup I had recovered.

"Is there anything I can do for you, captain?" I asked.

He mounted his horse, looked down at me. Then he gave me another of his rare smiles.

"No," he said, "at this moment there is nothing that you can do for *me*, thank you; but if you could give my boys a cup of tea, I imagine that you would just about save their lives." And nodding to me, he said to the picket, "This lady is kind enough to offer you a cup of tea," and he rode off, taking the road down the hill to Voisins.

I ran into the house, put on the kettle, ran up the road to call Amélie, and back to the arbour to set the table as well as I could. The whole atmosphere was changed. I was going to be useful.

I had no idea how many men I was going to feed. I had only seen three. To this day I don't know how many I did feed. They came and came and came. It reminded me of hens running toward a place when another hen has

found something good. It did not take me
many minutes to discover that these men needed
something more substantial than tea. Luckily
I had brought back from Paris an emergency
stock of things like biscuit, dry cakes, jam, etc.,
for even before our shops were closed there was
mighty little in them. For an hour and a half I
brewed pot after pot of tea, opened jar after jar
of jam and jelly, and tin after tin of biscuit and
cakes, and although it was hardly hearty fodder
for men, they put it down with a relish. I have
seen hungry men, but never anything as hungry
as these boys.

I knew little about military discipline—less
about the rules of active service; so I had no
idea that I was letting these hungry men—and
evidently hunger laughs at laws—break all the
regulations of the army. Their guns were lying
about in any old place; their kits were on the
ground; their belts were unbuckled. Suddenly
the captain rode up the road and looked over
the hedge at the scene. The men were sitting
on the benches, on the ground, anywhere, and
were all smoking my best Egyptian cigarettes,
and I was running round as happy as a queen,
seeing them so contented and comfortable.

It was a rude awakening when the captain
rode up the street.

There was a sudden jumping up, a hurried
buckling up of belts, a grab for kits and guns,
and an unceremonious cut for the gate. I heard

a volley from the officer. I marked a serious effort on the part of the men to keep the smiles off their faces as they hurriedly got their kits on their backs and their guns on their shoulders, and, rigidly saluting, dispersed up the hill, leaving two very straight men marching before the gate as if they never in their lives had thought of anything but picket duty.

The captain never even looked at me, but rode up the hill after his men. A few minutes later he returned, dismounted at the gate, tied his horse, and came in. I was a bit confused. But he smiled one of those smiles of his, and I got right over it.

"Dear little lady," he said, "I wonder if there is any tea left for me?"

Was there! I should think so; and I thought to myself, as I led the way into the dining-room, that he was probably just as hungry as his men.

While I was making a fresh brew he said to me:

"You must forgive my giving my men Hades right before you, but they deserved it, and know it, and under the circumstances I imagine they did not mind taking it. I did not mean you to give them a party, you know. Why, if the major had ridden up that hill—and he might have—and seen that party inside your garden, I should have lost my commission and those boys got the guardhouse. These men are on active service."

Then, while he drank his tea, he told me why he felt a certain indulgence for them—these boys who were hurried away from England without having a chance to take leave of their families, or even to warn them that they were going.

"This is the first time that they have had a chance to talk to a woman who speaks their tongue since they left England; I can't begrudge it to them and they know it. But discipline is discipline, and if I had let such a breach of it pass they would have no respect for me. They understand. They had no business to put their guns out of their hands. What would they have done if the detachment of Uhlans we are watching for had dashed up that hill—as they might have?"

Before I could answer or remark on this startling speech there was a tremendous explosion, which brought me to my feet, with the inevitable, "What's that?"

He took a long pull at his tea before he replied quietly, "Another division across the Marne."

Then he went on as if there had been no interruption:

"This Yorkshire regiment has had hard luck. Only one other regiment in the Expedition has had worse. They have marched from the Belgian frontier, and they have been in four big actions in the retreat—Mons, Cambrai, Saint-Quentin, and La Fère. Saint-Quentin was pretty rough luck. We went into the trenches a full regiment. We came out to retreat again with four hundred men—and I left my younger brother there."

I gasped; I could not find a word to say. He did not seem to feel it necessary that I should. He simply winked his eyelids, stiffened his stern mouth, and went right on; and I forgot all about the Uhlans:

"At La Fère we lost our commissary on the field. It was burned, and these lads have not had a decent feed since—that was three days ago. We have passed through few towns since, and those were evacuated,—drummed out; and fruit from the orchards on the roadsides is about all they have had—hardly good feed for a marching army in such hot weather. Besides, we were moving pretty fast—but in order—to get across the Marne, toward which we have been drawing the Germans, and in every one of these battles we have been fighting with one man to their ten."

I asked him where the Germans were.

"Can't say," he replied.

"And the French?"

"No idea. We've not seen them—yet. We understood that we were to be reinforced at Saint-Quentin by a French detachment at four o'clock. They got there at eleven—the battle was over—and lost. But these boys gave a wonderful account of themselves, and in spite of the disaster retreated in perfect order."

Then he told me that at the last moment he ordered his company to lie close in the trench and let the Germans come right up to them, and not to budge until he ordered them to give them what they hate—the bayonet. The Germans were within a few yards when a German automobile carrying a machine gun bore down on them and discovered their position, but the English sharpshooters picked off the five men the car carried before they could fire a shot, and after that it was every man for himself—what the French call "*sauve qui peut*."

The Uhlans came back to my mind, and it seemed to me a good time to ask him what he was doing here. Oddly enough, in spite of the several shocks I had had, and perhaps because of his manner, I was able to do it as if it was the sort of tea-table conversation to which I had always been accustomed.

"What are you doing here?" I said.

"Waiting for orders," he answered.

"And for Uhlans?"

"Oh," replied he, "if incidentally while we are sitting down here to rest, we could rout out a detachment of German cavalry, which our aeroplane tells us crossed the Marne ahead of us, we would like to. Whether this is one of those flying squads they are so fond of sending ahead, just to do a little terrorizing, or whether they escaped from the battle of La Fère, we don't know. I fancy the latter, as they do not seem to have done any harm or to have been too anxious to be seen."

I need not tell you that my mind was acting like lightning. I remembered, in the pause, as I poured him another cup of tea, and pushed the jam pot toward him, that Amélie had heard at Voisins last night that there were horses in the woods near the canal; that they had been heard neighing in the night; and that we had jumped to the conclusion that there were English cavalry there. I mentioned this to the captain, but for some reason it did not seem to make much impression on him; so I did not insist, as there was something that seemed more important which I had been getting up the courage to ask him. It had been on my lips all day. I put it.

"Captain," I asked, "do you think there is any danger in my staying here?"

He took a long drink before he answered:

"Little lady, there is danger everywhere between Paris and the Channel. Personally—since you have stayed until getting away will be difficult—I do not really believe that there is any reason why you should not stick it out. You may have a disagreeable time. But I honestly believe you are running no real risk of having more than that. At all events, I am going to do what I can to assure your personal safety. As we understand it—no one really *knows* anything except the orders given out—it is not intended that the Germans shall cross the Marne *here*. But who knows? Anyway, if I move on, each division of the Expeditionary Force that retreats to this hill will know that you are here. If it is necessary, later, for you to leave, you will be notified and precautions taken for your safety. You are not afraid?"

I could only tell him, "Not yet," but I could not help adding, "Of course I am not so stupid as to suppose for a moment that you English have retreated here to amuse yourselves, or that you have dragged your artillery up the hill behind me just to exercise your horses or to give your gunners a pretty promenade."

He threw back his head and laughed aloud for the first time, and I felt better.

"Precautions do not always mean a battle, you know"; and as he rose to his feet he called my attention to a hole in his coat, saying, "It was a miracle that I came through Saint-Quentin with a whole skin. The bullets simply rained about me. It was pouring—I had on a mackintosh— which made me conspicuous as an officer, if my height had not exposed me. Every German regiment carries a number of sharpshooters whose business is to pick off the officers. However, it was evidently not my hour."

As we walked out to the gate I asked him if there was anything else I could do for him.

"Do you think," he replied, "that you could

get me a couple of fresh eggs at half-past seven and let me have a cold wash-up?"

"Well, rather," I answered, and he rode away.

As soon as he was gone one of the picket called from the road to know if they could have "water and wash."

I told them of course they could—to come right in.

He said that they could not do that, but that if they could have water at the gate—and I did not mind—they could wash up in relays in the road. So Père came and drew buckets and buckets of water, and you never saw such a stripping and such a slopping, as they washed and shaved—and with such dispatch. They had just got through, luckily, when, at about half-past six, the captain rode hurriedly down the hill again. He carried a slip of white paper in his hand, which he seemed intent on deciphering.

As I met him at the gate he said:

"Sorry I shall miss those eggs—I've orders to move east"; and he began to round up his men.

I foolishly asked him why. I felt as if I were losing a friend.

"Orders," he answered. Then he put the slip of paper into his pocket, and leaning down he said:

"Before I go I am going to ask you to let my

corporal pull down your flags. You may think it cowardly. I think it prudent. They can be seen a long way. It is silly to wave a red flag at a bull. Any needless display of bravado on your part would be equally foolish."

So the corporal climbed up and pulled down the big flags, and together we marched them off to the stable. When I returned to the gate, where the captain was waiting for the rest of the picket to arrive, I was surprised to find my French caller of the morning standing there, with a pretty blonde girl, whom she introduced as her sister-in-law. She explained that they had started in the morning, but that their wagon had been overloaded and broken down and they had had to return, and that her mother was "glad of it." It was perfectly natural that she should ask me to ask the "English officer if it was safe to stay." I repeated the question. He looked down at them, asked if they were friends of mine. I explained that they were neighbours and acquaintances only.

"Well," he said, "I can only repeat what I said to you this morning—I think you are safe here. But for God's sake, don't give it to them as coming from me. I can assure your personal safety, but I cannot take the whole village on my conscience."

I told him that I would not quote him.

All this time he had been searching in a letter-case, and finally selected an envelope from which he removed the letter, passing me the empty cover.

"I want you," he said, "to write me a letter —that address will always reach me. I shall be anxious to know how you came through, and every one of these boys will be interested. You have given them the only happy day they have had since they left home. As for me—if I live —I shall sometime come back to see you. Good-bye and good luck." And he wheeled his horse and rode up the hill, his boys marching behind him; and at the turn of the road they all looked back and I waved my hand, and I don't mind telling you that I nodded to the French girls at the gate and got into the house as quickly as I could—and wiped my eyes. Then I cleared up the tea-mess. It was not until the house was in order again that I put on my glasses and read the envelope that the captain had given me:

*Capt. —— S——,*
    *King's Own Yorkshire L.I.*
        *13th Infantry Brigade,*
            *15th Division,*
                *British Expeditionary Force.*

And I put it carefully away in my address book until the time should come for me to write and tell "how I came through"; the phrase did disturb me a little.

I did not eat any supper. Food seemed to be

the last thing I wanted. I sat down in the study to read. It was about eight when I heard the gate open. Looking out I saw a man in khaki, his gun on his shoulder, marching up the path. I went to the door.

"Good evening, ma'am," he said. "All right?"

I assured him that I was.

"I am the corporal of the guard," he added. "The commander's compliments, and I was to report to you that your road was picketed for the night and that all is well."

I thanked him, and he marched away, and took up his post at the gate, and I knew that this was the commander's way of letting me know that Captain S—— had kept his word. I had just time while the corporal stood at the door to see "Bedford" on his cap, so I knew that the new regiment was from Bedfordshire.

I sat up awhile longer, trying to fix my mind on my book, trying not to look round constantly at my pretty green interior, at all my books, looking so ornamental against the walls of my study, at all the portraits of the friends of my life of active service above the shelves, and the old sixteenth-century Buddha, which Oda Neilson sent me on my last birthday, looking so stoically down from his perch to remind me how little all these things counted. I could not help remembering at the end that my friends at Voulangis had gone—that they were at that very

moment on their way to Marseilles, that almost
every one else I knew on this side of the water
was either at Havre waiting to sail, or in London,
or shut up in Holland or Denmark; that except for the friends I had at the front I was alone
with my beloved France and her Allies. Through
it all there ran a thought that made me laugh at
last—how all through August I had felt so outside of things, only suddenly to find it right at
my door. In the back of my mind—pushed back
as hard as I could—stood the question, What was
to become of all this?

Yet, do you know, I went to bed, and what
is more I slept well. I was physically tired.
The last thing I saw as I closed up the house was
the gleam of the moonlight on the muskets of
the picket pacing the road, and the first thing I
heard, as I waked suddenly at about four, was the
crunching of the gravel as they still marched there.

I got up at once. It was the morning of
Friday, the 4th of September. I dressed hurriedly,
ran down to put the kettle on, and start the
coffee, and by five o'clock I had a table spread
in the road, outside the gate, with hot coffee and
milk and bread and jam. I had my lesson, so I
called the corporal and explained that his men
were to come in relays, and when the coffee-pot
was empty there was more in the house; and I
left them to serve themselves, while I finished
dressing. I knew that the officers were likely to
come over, and one idea was fixed in my mind:

I must not look demoralized. So I put on a clean white frock, white shoes and stockings, a big black bow in my hair, and I felt equal to anything—in spite of the fact that before I dressed I heard far off a booming—could it be cannon? —and more than once a nearer explosion,— more bridges down, more English across.

It was not much after nine when two English officers strolled down the road—Captain E—— and Major A——, of the Bedfordshire Regiment. They came into the garden, and the scene with Captain S—— of the day before was practically repeated. They examined the plain, located the towns, looked long at it with their glasses; and that being over I put the usual question, " Can I do anything for you?" and got the usual answer, " Eggs."

I asked how many officers there were in the mess, and he replied " Five"; so I promised to forage, and away they went.

As soon as they were out of sight the picket set up a howl for baths. These Bedfordshire boys were not hungry, but they had retreated from their last battle leaving their kits in the trenches, and were without soap or towels, or combs or razors. But that was easily remedied. They washed up in relays in the court at Amélie's —it was a little more retired. As Amélie had put all her towels, etc., down underground, I ran back and forward between my house and hers for all sorts of things, and, as they slopped until the road ran tiny rivulets, I had to change shoes and stockings twice. I was not conscious till afterward how funny it all was. I must have been a good deal like an excited duck, and Amélie like a hen with a duckling. When she was not twitching my sash straight, she was run-about after me with dry shoes and stockings, and a chair, for fear "madame was getting too tired"; and when she was not doing that she was clapping my big garden hat on my head, for fear "madame would get a sunstroke." The joke was that I did not know it was hot. I did not even know it was funny until afterward, when the whole scene seemed to have been by a sort of dual process photographed unconsciously on my memory.

When the boys were all washed and shaved and combed,—and they were so larky over it,—we were like old friends. I did not know one of them by name, but I did know who was married, and who had children; and how one man's first child had been born since he left England, and no news from home because they had seen their mail wagon burn on the battle-field; and how one of them was only twenty, and had been six years in the army,—lied when he enlisted; how none of them had ever seen war before; how they had always wanted to, and "Now," said twenty-years old, "I've seen it—good Lord—and all I want is to get home," and he drew out of his breast pocket a photograph of a young girl in all her best clothes, sitting up very straight.

When I said, "Best girl?" he said proudly, "Only one, and we were to have been married in January if this hadn't happened. Perhaps we may yet, if we get home at Christmas, as they tell us we may."

I wondered who he meant by "they." The officers did not give any such impression.

While I was gathering up towels and things before returning to the house, this youngster advanced toward me, and said with a half-shy smile, "I take it you're a lady."

I said I was glad he had noticed it—I did make such an effort.

"No, no," he said, "I'm not joking. I may not say it very well, but I am quite serious. We all want to say to you that if it is war that makes you and the women you live amongst so different from English women, then all we can say is that the sooner England is invaded and knows what it means to have a fighting army on her soil, and see her fields devastated and her homes destroyed, the better it will be for the race. You take my word for it, they have no notion of what war is like; and there ain't no English woman of your class could have, or would have, done for us what you have done this morning. Why, in England the common soldier is the dirt under the feet of women like you."

I had to laugh, as I told him to wait and see how they treated them when war was there; that they probably had not done the thing simply because they never had had the chance.

"Well," he answered, "they'll have to change mightily. Why, our own women would have been uncomfortable and ashamed to see a lot of dirty men stripping and washing down like we have done. You haven't looked as if you minded it a bit, or thought of anything but getting us cleaned up as quick and comfortable as possible."

I started to say that I felt terribly flattered that I had played the rôle so well, but I knew he would not understand. Besides, I was wondering if it were true. I never knew the English except as individuals, never as a race. So I only laughed, picked up my towels, and went home to rest.

Just before noon a bicycle scout came over with a message from Captain E——, and I sent back by him a basket of eggs, a cold chicken, and a bottle of wine as a contribution to the breakfast at the officers' mess; and by the time I had eaten my breakfast, the picket had been changed, and I saw no more of those boys.

During the afternoon the booming off at the east became more distinct. It surely was cannon. I went out to the gate where the corporal of the guard was standing, and asked him, "Do I hear cannon?"

"You bet, you do," he replied.

"Do you know where it is?" I asked.

He said he hadn't an idea—about twenty-five or thirty miles away. And on he marched, up and down the road, perfectly indifferent to it.

When Amélie came to help get tea at the gate, she said that a man from Voisins, who had started with the crowd that left here Wednesday, had returned. He had brought back the news that the sight on the road was simply horrible. The *réfugiés* had got so blocked in their hurry that they could move in neither direction; cattle and horses were so tired that they fell by the way; it would take a general to disentangle them. My! wasn't I glad that I had not been tempted to get into that mess!

Just after the boys had finished their tea, Captain E——— came down the road, swinging my empty basket on his arm, to say "Thanks" for his breakfast. He looked at the table at the gate.

"So the men have been having tea—lucky men—and bottled water! What extravagance!"

"Come in and have some, too," I said.

"Love to," he answered, and in he came.

While I was making the tea he walked about the house, looked at the pictures, examined the books. Just as the table was ready there was a tremendous explosion. He went to the door, looked off, and remarked, as if it were the most natural thing in the world, "Another division across. That should be the last."

"Are all the bridges down?" I asked.

"All, I think, except the big railroad bridge behind you—Chalifert. That will not go until the last minute."

I wanted to ask, "When will it be the 'last minute'—and what does the 'last minute' mean?"—but where was the good? So we went into the dining-room. As he threw his hat on to a chair and sat down with a sigh, he said, "You see before you a very humiliated man. About half an hour ago eight of the Uhlans we are looking for rode right into the street below you, in Voisins. We saw them, but they got away. It is absolutely our own stupidity."

"Well," I explained to him, "I fancy I can tell you where they are hiding. I told Captain S—— so last night." And I explained to him that horses had been heard in the woods at the foot of the hill since Tuesday; that there was a cart road, rough and winding, running in toward Condé for over two miles; that it was absolutely screened by trees, had plenty of water, and not a house in it,—a shelter for a regiment of cavalry. And I had the impertinence to suggest that if the picket had been extended to the road below that it would have been impossible for the Germans to have got into Voisins.

"Not enough of us," he replied. "We are guarding a wide territory, and cannot put our pickets out of sight of one another." Then he explained that, as far as he knew from his aeroplane men, the detachment had broken up since it was first discovered on this side of the Marne. It was reported that there were only about twenty-four in this vicinity; that they were believed to be without ammunition; and then he dropped the subject, and I did not bother him with questions that were bristling in my mind.

He told me how sad it was to see the ruin of the beautiful country through which they had passed, and what a mistake it had been from his point of view not to have foreseen the methods of the Germans and drummed out all the towns through which the armies had passed. He told me one or two touching and interesting stories. One was of the day before a battle, I think it was Saint-Quentin. The officers had been invited to dine at a pretty château near which they had bivouacked. The French family could not do too much for them, and the daughters of the house waited at the table. Almost before the meal was finished the *alerte* sounded, and the battle was on them. When they retreated by the house where they had been so prettily entertained such a few hours before, there was not one stone standing on another, and what became of the family he had no idea.

The other that I remember was of the way the Germans passed the river at Saint-Quentin and forced the battle at La Fère on them. The bridge was mined, and the captain was standing beside the engineer waiting to give the order to touch off the mine. It was a nasty night—a Sunday (only last Sunday, think of that!)—and the rain was coming down in torrents. Just before the Germans reached the bridge he ordered it to be blown up. The engineer touched the button. The fuse did not act. He was in despair, but the captain said to him, "Brace up, my lad—give her another chance." The second effort failed like the first. Then, before any one could stop him, the engineer made a dash for the end of the bridge, drawing his revolver as he ran, and fired six shots into the mine, knowing that, if he succeeded, he would go up with the bridge. No good, and he was literally dragged off the spot weeping with rage at his failure—and the Germans came across.

All the time we had been talking I had heard the cannonade in the distance—now at the north and now in the east. This seemed a proper moment, inspired by the fact that he was talking war, of his own initiative, to put a question or two, so I risked it.

"That cannonading seems much nearer than it did this morning," I ventured.

"Possibly," he replied.

"What does that mean?" I persisted.

"Sorry I can't tell you. We men know absolutely nothing. Only three men in this war know anything of its plans,—Kitchener, Joffre, and French. The rest of us obey orders, and know only what we see. Not even a brigade commander is any wiser. Once in a while the colonel makes a remark, but he is never illuminating."

"How much risk am I running by remaining here?"

He looked at me a moment before he asked, "You want to know the truth?"

"Yes," I replied.

"Well, this is the situation as near as I can work it out. We infer from the work we were given to do—destroying bridges, railroads, telegraphic communications—that an effort is to be made here to stop the march on Paris; in fact, that the Germans are not to be allowed to cross the Marne at Meaux, and march on the city by the main road from Rheims to the capital. The communications are all cut. That does not mean that it will be impossible for them to pass; they've got clever engineers. It means that we have impeded them and may stop them. I don't know. Just now your risk is nothing. It will be nothing unless we are ordered to hold this hill, which is the line of march from Meaux to Paris. We have had no such order yet. But if the Germans succeed in taking Meaux and attempt to put their bridges across the Marne, our artillery, behind you there on the top of the hill, must open fire on them over your head. In that case the Germans will surely reply by bombarding this hill." And he drank his tea without looking to see how I took it.

I remember that I was standing opposite him, and I involuntarily leaned against the wall behind me, but suddenly thought, "Be careful. You'll break the glass in the picture of Whistler's Mother, and you'll be sorry." It brought me up standing, and he didn't notice. Isn't the mind a queer thing?

He finished his tea, and rose to go. As he picked up his cap he showed me a hole right through his sleeve—in one side, out the other—and a similar one in his puttee, where the ball had been turned aside by the leather lacing of his boot. He laughed as he said, "Odd how near a chap comes to going out, and yet lives to drink tea with you. Well, good-bye and good luck if I don't see you again."

And off he marched, and I went into the library and sat down and sat very still.

It was not more than half an hour after Captain E—— left that the corporal came in to ask me if I had a window in the roof. I told him that there was, and he asked if he might go up. I led the way, picking up my glasses as I went. He explained, as we climbed the two flights of stairs, that the aeroplane had reported a part of the Germans they were hunting "not a thousand feet from this house." I opened the skylight. He scanned in every direction. I knew he would not see anything, and he did not. But he seemed to like the view, could command the roads that his posse was guarding, so he sat on the window ledge and talked. The common soldier is far fonder of talking than his officer and apparently he knows more. If he doesn't, he thinks he does. So he explained to me the situation as the "men saw it." I remembered what Captain Edwards had told me, but I listened all the same. He told me that the Germans were advancing in two columns about ten miles apart, flanked in the west by a French division pushing them east, and led by the English drawing them toward the Marne. "You know," he said, "that we are the sacrificed corps, and we have known it from the first—went into the campaign knowing it. We have been fighting a force ten times superior in numbers, and retreating, doing rear-guard action, whether we were really outfought or not—to draw the Germans where Joffre wants them. I reckon we've got them there. It is great strategy —Kitchener's, you know."

Whether any of the corporal's ideas had any relation to facts I shall never know until history tells me, but I can assure you that, as I followed the corporal downstairs, I looked about my house—and, well, I don't deny it, it seemed to me a doomed thing, and I was sorry for it. However, as I let him out into the road again, I pounded into myself lots of things like " It hasn't happened yet"; "Sufficient unto the

day"; and, "What isn't to be, won't be "; and
found I was quite calm. Luckily I did not have
much time to myself, for I had hardly sat down
quietly when there was another tap at the door
and I opened it to find an officer of the bicycle
corps standing there.

"Captain E——'s compliments," he said,
"and will you be so kind as to explain to me
exactly where you think the Uhlans are hidden?"

I told him that if he would come down the
road a little way with me I would show him.

"Wait a moment," he said, holding the door.
"You are not afraid?"

I told him that I was not.

"My orders are not to expose you uselessly.
Wait there a minute."

He stepped back into the garden, gave a
quick look overhead,—I don't know what for,
unless for a Taube. Then he said, "Now, you
will please come out into the road and keep
close to the bank at the left, in the shadow. I
shall walk at the extreme right. As soon as I get
where I can see the roads ahead, at the foot of
the hill, I shall ask you to stop, and please stop
at once. I don't want you to be seen from the
road below, in case any one is there. Do you
understand?"

I said I did. So we went into the road and
walked silently down the hill. Just before we
got to the turn, he motioned me to stop and

stood with his map in hand while I explained that he was to cross the road that led into Voisins, take the cart track down the hill past the washhouse on his left, and turn into the wood road on that side. At each indication he said, " I have it." When I had explained, he simply said, " Rough road ? "

I said it was, very, and wet in the dryest weather.

" Wooded all the way ? " he asked.

I told him that it was, and, what was more, so winding that you could not see ten feet ahead anywhere between here and Condé.

"Humph," he said. "Perfectly clear, thank you very much. Please wait just there a moment."

He looked up the hill behind him, and made a gesture in the air with his hand above his head. I turned to look up the hill also. I saw the corporal at the gate repeat the gesture ; then a big bicycle corps, four abreast, guns on their backs, slid round the corner and came gliding down the hill. There was not a sound, not the rattle of a chain or a pedal.

" Thank you very much," said the captain. " Be so kind as to keep close to the bank."

When I reached my gate I found some of the men of the guard dragging a big, long log down the road, and I watched them while they attached it to a tree at my gate, and swung it across to the opposite side of the road, making in that way a barrier about five feet high. I asked what that was for? "Captain's orders," was the laconic reply. But when it was done the corporal took the trouble to explain that it was a barricade to prevent the Germans from making a dash up the hill.

"However," he added, "don't you get nervous. If we chase them out it will only be a little rifle practice, and I doubt if they even have any ammunition."

As I turned to go into the house, he called after me,—

"See here, I notice that you've got doors on all sides of your house. Better lock all those but this front one."

As all the windows were barred and so could be left open, I didn't mind; so I went in and locked up. The thing was getting to be funny to me,—always doing something, and nothing happening. I suppose courage is a cumulative thing, if only one has time to accumulate, and these boys in khaki treated even the cannon-ading as if it were all "in the day's work."

It was just dusk when the bicycle corps returned up the hill. They had to dismount and wheel their machines under the barricade, and they did it so prettily, dismounting and re-mounting with a precision that was neat.

"Nothing," reported the captain. "We could not go in far,—road too rough and too dangerous. It is a cavalry job."

All the same, I am sure the Uhlans are there.

# XIII

*September* 6, 1914.

I HAD gone to bed early on Friday night, and had passed an uneasy night. It was before four when I got up and opened my shutters. It was a lovely day. Perhaps I have told you that the weather all last week was simply perfect.

I went downstairs to get coffee for the picket, but when I got out to the gate there was no picket there. There was the barricade, but the road was empty. I ran up the road to Amélie's. She told me that they had marched away about an hour before. A bicyclist had evidently brought an order. As no one spoke English, no one understood what had really happened. Père had been to Couilly—they had all left there. So far as any one could discover there was not an English soldier, or any kind of a soldier, left anywhere in the commune.

This was Saturday morning, September 5, and one of the loveliest days I ever saw. The air was clear. The sun was shining. The birds were singing. But otherwise it was very still. I walked out on the lawn. Little lines of white smoke were rising from a few chimneys at Joncheroy and Voisins. The towns on the plain, from Monthyon and Penchard on the horizon to Mareuil in the valley, stood out clear and distinct. But after three days of activity, three days with the soldiers about, it seemed, for the first time since I came here, lonely; and for the first time I realized that I was actually cut off from the outside world. All the bridges in front of me were gone, and the big bridge behind me. No communication possible with the north, and none with the south except by road over the hill to Lagny. Esbly evacuated, Couilly evacuated, Quincy evacuated. All the shops closed. No government, no post-office, and absolutely no knowledge of what had happened since Wednesday. I had a horrible sense of isolation.

Luckily for me, part of the morning was killed by what might be called an incident or a disaster or a farce—just as you look at it. First of all, right after breakfast I had the proof that I was right about the Germans. Evidently well informed of the movements of the English, they rode boldly into the open. Luckily they seemed disinclined to do any mischief. Perhaps the place looked too humble to be bothered with. They simply asked—one of them spoke French, and perhaps they all did—where they were, and were told, "Huiry, commune of Quincy." They looked it up on their maps, nodded, and asked if the bridges on the Marne had been destroyed, to which I replied that I did not know,—I had not been down to the river. Half a truth and half a lie, but goodness knows that it was hard enough to have to be polite. They thanked me civilly enough and rode down the hill, as they could not pass the barricade unless they had wished to give an exhibition of " high school." Wherever they had been they had not suffered. Their horses were fine animals, and both horses and men were well groomed and in prime condition.

The other event was distressing, but about that I held my tongue.

Just after the Germans were here, I went down the road to call on my new French friends at the foot of the hill, to hear how they had passed the night, and incidentally to discover if there were any soldiers about. Just in front of their house I found an English bicycle scout, leaning on his wheel and trying to make himself understood in a one-sided monosyllabic dialogue, with the two girls standing in their window.

I asked him who he was. He showed his papers. They were all right—an Irishman— thirteen years in the service.

I asked him if there were any English soldiers left here.

He said there was still a bicycle corps of scouts at the foot of the hill, at Couilly. I thought that funny, as Père had said the town was absolutely deserted. Still, I saw no reason to doubt his word, so when he asked me if I could give him his breakfast, I brought him back to the house, set the table in the arbour, and gave him his coffee and eggs. When he had finished, he showed no inclination to go—said he would rest a bit. As Amélie was in the house, I left him, and went back to make the call my encounter with him had interrupted. When I returned an hour later, I found him fast asleep on the bench in the arbour, with the sun shining right on his head. His wheel, with his kit and gun on it, was leaning up against the house.

It was nearly noon by this time, and hot, and I was afraid he would get a sunstroke; so I waked him and told him that if it was a rest he needed,—and he was free to take it—he could go into the room at the head of the stairs, where he would find a couch and lie down comfortably. He had sleepily obeyed, and must have just about got to sleep again, when it occurred to me that it was hardly prudent to leave an English bicycle with a khaki-covered kit and a gun on it right on the terrace in plain sight of the road up which the Germans had ridden so short a time before. So I went to the foot of the stairs, called him, and explained that I did not care to touch the wheel on account of the gun, so he had better come down and put it away, which he did. I don't know whether it was my saying " Germans " to him that explained it, but his sleepiness seemed suddenly to have disappeared, so he asked for the chance to wash and shave; and half an hour later he came down all slicked up and spruce, with a very visible intention of paying court to the lady of the house. Irish, you see,—white hairs no obstacle.

I could not help laughing. " Hoity-toity," I said to myself, " I am getting all kinds of impressions of the military."

" While I was, with amusement, putting up fences, the gardener next door came down the hill in great excitement to tell me that the Germans were on the road above, and were riding down across Père's farm into a piece of land called "*la terre blanche*," where Père had recently been digging out great rocks, making it an ideal place to hide. He knew that there was an English scout in my house and thought I ought to know. I suppose he expected the boy in khaki to grab his gun and capture them all. I thanked him and sent him away. I must say my Irishman did not seem a bit interested in the Germans. His belt and pistol lay on the salon table, where he put them when he came downstairs. He made himself comfortable in an easy chair, and continued to give me another dose of his blarney. I suppose I was getting needlessly nervous. It was really none of my business what he was doing here. Still he was a bit too *sans gêne*.

Finally he began to ask questions. " Was I afraid?" I was not. " Did I live alone?" I did. As soon as I had said it, I thought it was

stupid of me, especially as he at once said,—
"If you are, yer know, I'll come back here to
sleep to-night. I'm perfectly free to come and
go as I like,—don't have to report until I'm
ready."

I thought it wise to remind him right here
that if his corps was at the foot of the hill, it
was wise for him to let his commanding officer
know that the Germans, for whom two regiments
had been hunting for three days, had come out
of hiding. I fancy if I had not taken that tack
he'd have settled for the day.

"Put that thing on," I said, pointing to his
pistol; "get your wheel out of the barn, and
I'll take a look up the road and see that it's
clear. I don't care to see you attacked under
my eyes."

I knew that there was not the slightest danger
of that, but it sounded business-like. I am afraid
he found it so, because he said at once, "Could
you give me a drink before I go?"

"Water?" I said.

"No, not that."

I was going to say "no" when it occurred to
me that Amélie had told me that she had put a
bottle of cider in the buffet, and—well, he was
Irish, and I wanted to get rid of him. So I said
he could have a glass of cider, and I got the
bottle, and a small, deep champagne glass. He
uncorked the bottle, filled a brimming glass,
recorked the bottle, drank it off, and thanked

me more earnestly than cider would have seemed to warrant. While he got his wheel out I went through the form of making sure the road was free. There was no one in sight. So I sent him away with directions for reaching Couilly without going over the part of the hill where the Uhlans had ridden, and drew a sigh of relief when he was off. Hardly fifteen minutes later someone came running up from Voisins to tell me that just round the corner he had slipped off his wheel, almost unconscious,—evidently drunk. I was amazed. He had been absolutely all right when he left me. As no one understood a word he tried to say, there was nothing to do but go and rescue him. But by the time I got to where he had fallen off his wheel, he was gone,—some one had taken him away,—and it was not until later that I knew the truth of the matter, but that must keep until I get to the way of the discovery.

All this excitement kept me from listening too much to the cannon, which had been booming ever since nine o'clock. Amélie had been busy running between her house and mine, but she has, among other big qualities, the blessed habit of taking no notice. I wish it were contagious. She went about her work as if nothing were hanging over us. I walked about the house doing little things aimlessly. I don't believe Amélie shirked a thing. It seemed to me absurd to care whether the dusting were done or not, whether or not the writing-table was in order, or the pictures straight on the wall.

As near as I can remember, it was a little after one o'clock when the cannonading suddenly became much heavier, and I stepped out into the orchard, from which there is a wide view of the plain. I gave one look; then I heard myself say, "Amélie,"—as if she could help,—and I retreated. Amélie rushed by me. I heard her say, "Mon Dieu." I waited, but she did not come back. After a bit I pulled myself together, went out again, and followed down to the hedge where she was standing, looking off to the plain.

The battle had advanced right over the crest of the hill. The sun was shining brilliantly on silent Mareuil and Chauconin, but Monthyon and Penchard were enveloped in smoke. From the eastern and western extremities of the plain we could see the artillery fire, but owing to the smoke hanging over the crest of the hill on the horizon, it was impossible to get an idea of the positions of the armies. In the west it seemed to be somewhere near Claye, and in the east it was in the direction of Barcy. I tried to remember what the English soldiers had said,—that the Germans were, if possible, to be pushed east, in which case the artillery at the west must be either the French or English. The hard thing to bear was, that it was all conjecture.

So often, when I first took this place on the hill, I had looked off at the plain and thought,

"What a battlefield," forgetting how often the Seine et Marne had been that from the days when the kings lived at Chelles down to the days when it saw the worst of the invasion of 1870. But when I thought that, I had visions very different from what I was seeing. I had imagined long lines of marching soldiers, detachments of flying cavalry, like the war pictures at Versailles and Fontainebleau. Now I was actually seeing a battle, and it was nothing like that. There was only noise, belching smoke, and long drifts of white clouds concealing the hill.

By the middle of the afternoon Monthyon came slowly out of the smoke. That seemed to mean that the heaviest firing was over the hill and not on it,—or did it mean that the battle was receding? If it did, then the Allies were retreating. There was no way to discover the truth. And all this time the cannon thundered in the south-east, in the direction of Coulommiers, on the route into Paris by Ivry.

Naturally I could not but remember that we were only seeing the action on the extreme west of a battle-line which probably extended hundreds of miles. I had been told that Joffre had made a frontier of the Marne. But alas, the Meuse had been made a frontier—but the Germans had crossed it, and advanced to here in little less than a fortnight. If that—why not here? It was not encouraging.

A dozen times during the afternoon I went

into the study and tried to read. Little groups of old men, women, and children were in the road, mounted on the barricade which the English had left. I could hear the murmur of their voices. In vain I tried to stay indoors. The thing was stronger than I, and in spite of myself, I would go out on the lawn and, field-glass in hand, watch the smoke. To my imagination every shot meant awful slaughter, and between me and the terrible thing stretched a beautiful country, as calm in the sunshine as if horrors were not. In the field below me the wheat was being cut. I remembered vividly afterward that a white horse was drawing the reaper, and women and children were stacking and gleaning. Now and then the horse would stop, and a woman, with her red handkerchief on her head, would stand, shading her eyes a moment, and look off. Then the white horse would turn and go plodding on. The grain had to be got in if the Germans were coming, and these fields were to be trampled as they were in 1870. Talk about the duality of the mind—it is sextuple. I would not dare tell you all that went through mine that long afternoon.

It was just about six o'clock when the first bomb that we could really see came over the hill. The sun was setting. For two hours we saw them rise, descend, explode. Then a little smoke would rise from one hamlet, then from another; then a tiny flame—hardly more than a spark—would be visible; and by dark the whole plain was on fire, lighting up Mareuil in the foreground, silent and untouched. There were long lines of grain-stacks and mills stretching along the plain. One by one they took fire, until, by ten o'clock, they stood like a procession of huge torches across my beloved panorama.

It was midnight when I looked off for the last time. The wind had changed. The fires were still burning. The smoke was drifting toward us—and oh! the odour of it! I hope you will never know what it is like.

I was just going to close up when Amélie came to the door to see if I was all right. My mind was in a sort of riot. It was the suspense—the not knowing the result, or what the next day might bring. You know, I am sure, that physical fear is not one of my characteristics. Fear of Life, dread of Fate, I often have, but not the other. Yet somehow, when I saw Amélie standing there, I felt that I needed the sense of something living near me. So I said, " Amélie, do you want to do me a great service? "

She said she'd like to try.

" Well, then," I replied, " don't you want to sleep here to-night? "

With her pretty smile, she pulled her night-dress from under her arm : that was what she had come for. So I made her go to bed in the big bed in the guest-chamber, and leave the door wide open; and do you know, she was fast asleep in five minutes, and she snored, and I smiled to hear her, and thought it the most comforting sound I had ever heard.

As for me, I did not sleep a moment. I could not forget the poor fellows lying dead out there in the starlight—and it was such a beautiful night.

# XIV

*September* 7, 1914.

IT was about my usual time, four o'clock, the
next morning,—Sunday, September 6,—that
I opened my blinds. Another lovely day. I was
dressed and downstairs when, a little before five,
the battle recommenced.

I rushed out on the lawn and looked off. It
had moved east—behind the hill between me and
Meaux. All I could see was the smoke which
hung over it. Still it seemed nearer than it had
the day before. I had just about room enough
in my mind for one idea—" The Germans wish
to cross the Marne at Meaux, on the direct route
into Paris. They are getting there. In that case
to-day will settle our fate. If they reach the
Marne, that battery at Coutevroult will come
into action,"—that was what Captain E——
had said,—" and I shall be in a direct line between the two armies."

Amélie got breakfast as if there were no
cannon, so I took my coffee, and said nothing.
As soon as it was cleared away, I went up into
the attic, and quietly packed a tiny square hat-
trunk. I was thankful that this year's clothes
take up so little room. I put in changes of under-

130

wear, stockings, slippers, an extra pair of low-heeled shoes, plenty of handkerchiefs,—just the essentials in the way of toilette stuff,—a few bandages and such emergency things, and had room for two dresses. When it was packed and locked, it was so light that I could easily carry it by its handle on top. I put my long black military cape, which I could carry over my shoulder, on it, with hat and veil and gloves. Then I went downstairs and shortened the skirt of my best walking-suit, and hung it and its jacket handy. I was ready to fly,—if I had to, —and in case of that emergency had nothing to do for myself.

I had got all this done systematically when my little French friend—I call her Mlle. Henriette now—came to the door to say that she simply " could *not* stand another day of it." She had put, she said, all the ready money they had inside her corset, and a little box which contained all her dead father's decorations also, and she was ready to go. She took out the box and showed the pretty jewelled things,—his cross of the *Légion d'Honneur*, his Papal decoration, and several foreign orders,—her father, it seems, was an officer in the army, a great friend of the Orléans family, and grandson of an officer of Louis XVI's Imperial Guard. She begged me to join them in an effort to escape to the south. I told her frankly that it seemed to me impossible, and I felt it safer to wait until the English

officers at Coutevroult notified us that it was
necessary. It would be as easy then as now—
and I was sure that it was safer to wait for their
advice than to adventure it for ourselves. Besides, I had no intention of leaving my home
and all the souvenirs of my life without making
every effort I could to save them up to the last
moment. In addition to that, I could not see
myself joining that throng of homeless *réfugiés*
on the road, if I could help it.

"But," she insisted, "you cannot save your
house by staying. We are in the same position.
Our house is full of all the souvenirs of my
father's family. It is hard to leave all that—but
I am afraid—terribly afraid for the children."

I could not help asking her how she proposed
to get away. So far as I knew there was not a
carriage to be had.

She replied that we could start on foot in the
direction of Melun, and perhaps find an automobile : we could share the expense. Together
we could find a way, and what was more, that I
could share my optimism and courage with them
and that would help.

That made me laugh, but I didn't think it
necessary to explain to her that, once away
from the shelter of my own walls, I should be
just as liable to a panic as any one else, or that
I knew we should not find a conveyance, or,
worse still, that her money and her jewels would
hardly be safe inside her corset if she were to

meet with some of the Uhlans who were still
about us. Amélie had not allowed me to carry a
sou on me, nor even my handbag since we
knew they were here. Such things as that have
been hidden—all ready to be snatched up—ever
since I came home from Paris last Wednesday
—only four days ago, after all!

Poor Mlle. Henriette went away sadly when
she was convinced that my mind was made up.

" Good-bye," she called over the hedge. " I
seem to be always taking leave of you."

I did not tell Amélie anything about this conversation. What was the good? I fancy it
would have made no difference to her. I knew
pretty well to what her mind was made up.
Nothing in the world would have made Père
budge. He had tried it in 1870, and had been
led to the German post with a revolver at his
head. He did not have any idea of repeating
the experience. It was less than half an hour
later that Mlle. Henriette came up the hill again.
She was between tears and laughter.

" Mother will *not* go," she said. " She says if
you can stay we must. She thinks that staying
is the lesser of two evils. We can hide the babies
in the cave if necessary, and they may be as safe
there as on the road."

I could not help saying that I should be sorry
if my decision influenced theirs. I could be re-
sponsible for myself. I could not bear to have
to feel any responsibility for others in case I was

wrong. But she assured me that her mother had been of my opinion from the first. "Only," she added, " if I could have coaxed you to go, she would have gone too."

This decision did not add much to my peace of mind all that long Sunday. It seems impossible that it was only the day before yesterday. I think the suspense was harder to bear than that of the day before, though all we could see of the battle were the dense clouds of smoke rising straight into the air behind the green hill under such a blue sky all aglow with sunshine, with the incessant booming of the cannon, which made the contrasts simply monstrous.

I remember that it was about four in the afternoon when I was sitting in the arbour under the crimson rambler, which was a glory of bloom, that Père came and stood near by on the lawn, looking off. With his hands in the pockets of his blue apron, he stood silent for a long time. Then he said, " Listen to that. They are determined to pass. This is different from 1870. In 1870 the Germans marched through here with their guns on their shoulders. There was no one to oppose them. This time it is different. It was harvest-time that year, and they took everything, and destroyed what they did not take. They bedded their horses in the wheat."

You see Père's father was in the Franco-Prussian War, and his grandfather was with Napoleon at Moscow, where he had his feet frozen. Père is over seventy, and his father died at ninety-six. Poor old Père just hates the war. He is as timid as a bird—can't kill a rabbit for his dinner. But with the queer spirit of the French farmer he has kept right on working as if nothing were going on. All day Saturday and all day Sunday he was busy digging stone to mend the road.

The cannonading ceased a little after six— thirteen hours without intermission. I don't mind confessing to you that I hope the war is not going to give me many more days like that one. I'd rather the battle would come right along and be done with it. The suspense of waiting all day for that battery at Coutevroult to open fire was simply nasty.

I went to bed as ignorant of how the battle had turned as I was the night before. Oddly enough, to my surprise, I slept, and slept well.

## XV

I DID not wake on the morning of Monday, September 7,—yesterday,—until I was waked by the cannon at five. I jumped out of bed and rushed to the window. This time there could be no doubt of it: the battle was receding. The cannonading was as violent, as incessant, as it had been the day before, but it was surely farther off—to the north-east of Meaux. It was another beautiful day. I never saw such weather.

Amélie was on the lawn when I came down. "They are surely retreating," she called as soon as I appeared.

"They surely are," I replied. "It looks as if they were somewhere near Lizy-sur-l'Ourcq," and that was a guess of which I was proud a little later. I carry a map around these days as if I were an army officer.

As Amélie had not been for the milk the night before, she started off quite gaily for it. She has to go to the other side of Voisins. It takes her about half an hour to go and return; so—just for the sake of doing something—I thought I would run down the hill and see how Mlle. Henriette and the little family had got through the night.

# A HILLTOP ON THE MARNE

Amélie had taken the road across the fields. It is rough walking, but she doesn't mind. I had stopped to tie a fresh ribbon about my cap, —a tricolor,—and was about five minutes behind her. I was about half-way down the hill when I saw Amélie coming back, running, stumbling, waving her milk-can and shouting, " *Madame— un anglais, un anglais.*" And sure enough, coming on behind her, his face wreathed in smiles, was an English bicycle scout, wheeling his machine. As soon as he saw me, he waved his cap, and Amélie breathlessly explained that she had said, " *Dame américaine,*" and he had dismounted and followed her at once.

We went together to meet him. As soon as he was near enough, he called out, " Good morning. Everything is all right. Germans have been as near you as they will ever get. Close shave."

" Where are they?" I asked as we met.

" Retreating to the north-east—on the Ourcq."

I could have kissed him. Amélie did. She simply threw both arms round his neck and smacked him on both cheeks, and he said, " Thank you, ma'am," quite prettily; and, like the nice clean English boy he was, he blushed.

" You can be perfectly calm," he said. " Look behind you."

I looked, and there along the top of my hill I saw a long line of bicyclists in khaki.

"What are you doing here?" I asked, a little alarmed. For a moment I thought that if the English had returned, something was going to happen right here.

"English scouts," he replied. "Colonel S——'s division, clearing the way for the advance. You've a whole corps of fresh French troops coming out from Paris on one side of you, and the English troops are on their way to Meaux."

"But the bridges are down," I said.

"The pontoons are across. Everything is ready for the advance. I think we've got 'em." And he laughed as if it were all a game of cricket.

By this time we were in the road. I sent Amélie on for the milk. He wheeled his machine up the hill beside me. He asked me if there was anything they could do for me before they moved on. I told him there was nothing unless he could drive out the Uhlans who were hidden near us.

He looked a little surprised, asked a few questions—how long they had been there? where they were? how many? and if I had seen them? and I explained.

"Well," he said, "I'll speak to the colonel about it. Don't you worry. If he has time he may get over to see you, but we are moving pretty fast."

By this time we were at the gate. He stood

leaning on his wheel a moment, looking over
the hedge.

"Live here with your daughter?" he asked.

I told him that I lived here alone with myself.

"Wasn't that your daughter I met?"

I didn't quite fall through the gate backwards.
I am accustomed to saying that I am old. I am
not yet accustomed to have people notice it
when I do not call their attention to it. Amélie
is only ten years younger than I am, but she
has got the figure and bearing of a girl. The lad
recovered himself at once, and said, "Why, of
course not,—she doesn't speak any English." I
was glad that he didn't even apologize, for I
expect that I look fully a hundred and something. So with a reiterated "Don't worry—you
are all safe here now," he mounted his wheel
and rode up the hill.

I watched him making good time across to
the route to Meaux. Then I came into the
house and lay down. I suddenly felt horribly
weak. My house had taken on a queer look to
me. I suppose I had been, in a sort of subcon-
scious way, sure that it was doomed. As I lay
on the couch in the salon and looked round the
room, it suddenly appeared to me like a thing I
had loved and lost and recovered—resurrected,
in fact; a living thing to which a miracle had
happened. I even found myself asking, in my
innermost soul, what I had done to deserve this

fortune. How had it happened, and why, that I had come to perch on this hillside, just to see a battle, and have it come almost to my door, to turn back and leave me and my belongings standing here untouched, as safe as if there were no war,—and so few miles away destruction extending to the frontier.

The sensation was uncanny. Out there in the north-east still boomed the cannon. The smoke of the battle still rose straight in the still air. I had seen the war. I had watched its destructive bombs. For three days its cannon had pounded on every nerve in my body; but none of the horror it had sowed from the eastern frontier of Belgium to within four miles of me, had reached me except in the form of a threat. Yet out there on the plain, almost within my sight, lay the men who had paid with their lives —each dear to some one—to hold back the battle from Paris—and incidentally from me. The relief had its bitterness, I can tell you. I had been prepared to play the whole game. I had not even had the chance to discover whether or not I could. You, who know me fairly well, will see the irony of it. I am eternally hanging round *dans les coulisses*, I am never in the play. I instinctively thought of Captain S——, who had left his brother in the trenches at Saint-Quentin, and still had in him the kindly sympathy that had helped me so much.

When Amélie returned, she said that ev ry

one was out at the Demi-Lune to watch the
troops going to Meaux, and that the boys in
the neighbourhood were already swimming the
Marne to climb the hill to the battlefield of
Saturday. I had no curiosity to see one scene
or the other. I knew what the French boys were
like, with their stern faces, as well as I knew the
English manner of going forward to the day's
work, and the hilarious, *macabre* spirit of the
French untried lads crossing the river to look
on horrors as if it were a lark.

I passed a strangely quiet morning. But the
excitement was not all over. It was just after
lunch that Amélie came running down the road
to say that we were to have a *cantonnement de
régiment* on our hill for the night and perhaps
longer—French reinforcements marching out
from the south of Paris; that they were already
coming over the crest of the hill to the south
and could be seen from the road above; that the
advance scouts were already here. Before she
had done explaining, an officer and a bicyclist were
at the gate. I suppose they came here because
it was the only house on the road that was open.
I had to encounter the expressions of astonish-
ment to which I am now quite accustomed—a
foreigner in a little hole on the road to the
frontier, in a partially evacuated contry. I answered all the usual questions politely, but when
he began to ask how many men I could lodge,
and how much room there was for horses in the

outbuildings, Amélie sharply interfered, assuring him that she knew the resources of the hamlet better than I did, that she was used to " this sort of thing " and " madame was not "; and simply whisked him off.

I can assure you that, as I watched the work of billeting a regiment in evacuated houses, I was mighty glad that I was here, standing, a willing hostess, at my door, but giving to my little house a personality no unoccupied house can ever have to a passing army. They made quick work, and no ceremony, in opening locked doors and taking possession. It did not take the officer who had charge of the billeting half an hour, notebook in hand, to find quarters for his horses as well as his men. Before the head of the regiment appeared over the hill names were chalked up on all the doors, and the number of horses on every door to barn and courtyard, and the fields selected and the number of men to be camped all over the hill. Finally the officer returned to me. I knew by his manner that Amélie, who accompanied him, had been giving him a " talking to."

" If you please, madame," he said, "I will see now what you can do for us "; and I invited him in.

I don't suppose I need to tell you that you would get very little idea of the inside of my house from the outside. I am quite used now to the little change of front in most people when they cross the threshold. The officer nearly went on tiptoes when he got inside. He mounted the polished stairs gingerly, gave one look at the bedroom part-way up, touched his cap, and said: "That will do for the *chef-major*. We will not trouble you with anyone else. He has his own orderly, and will eat outside, and will be no bother. Thank you very much, madame"; and he sort of slid down the stairs, tiptoed out, and wrote in chalk on the gatepost, "Weitzel."

By this time the advanced guard was in the road and I could not resist going out to talk to them. They had marched out from the south of Paris since the day before—thirty-six miles— without an idea that the battle was going on on the Marne until they crossed the hill at Montry and came in sight of its smoke. I tell you their faces were wreathed with smiles when they discovered that we knew the Germans were retreating.

Such talks as I listened to that afternoon— only yesterday—at my gate, from such a fluent, amusing, clever French chap—a bicyclist in the ambulance corps—of the crossing the Meuse and the taking, losing, re-taking, and re-losing of Charleroi. Oddly enough these were the first real battle tales I had heard.

It suddenly occurred to me, as we chatted and laughed, that all the time the English were here they had never once talked battles. Not one of the Tommies had mentioned the fighting. We had talked of "home," of the girls they had left behind them, of the French children whom the English loved, of the country, its customs, its people, their courage and kindness, but not one had told me a battle story of any kind, and I had not once thought of opening the subject. But this French lad of the ambulance corps, with his Latin eloquence and his national gift of humour and graphic description, with a smile in his eyes, and a laugh on his lips, told me stories that made me see how war affects men, and how often the horrible passes across the line into the grotesque. I shall never forget him as he stood at the gate, leaning on his wheel, describing how the Germans crossed the Meuse —a feat which cost them so dearly that only their superior number made a victory out of a disaster.

"I suppose," he said, "that in the history of the war it will stand as a success—at any rate, they came across, which was what they wanted. We could only have stopped them, if at all, by an awful sacrifice of life. Joffre is not doing that. If the Germans want to fling away their men by the tens of thousands—let them. In the end we gain by it. We can rebuild a country; we cannot so easily re-create a race. We mowed them down like a field of wheat, by the tens of thousands, and tens of thousands sprang into the gaps. They advanced shoulder to shoulder. Our guns could not miss them, but they were too many for us. If you had seen that crossing I imagine it would have looked to you like a disaster for Germany. It was so awful that it became comic. I remember one point where a bridge was mined. We let the first divisions of artillery and cavalry come right across on to our guns—they were literally destroyed. As the next division came on to the bridge—up it went—men, horses, guns dammed the flood, and the cavalry literally crossed on their own dead. We are bold enough, but we are not so foolhardy as to throw away men like that. They will be more useful to Joffre later."

It was the word "comic" that did for me. There was no sign in the fresh young face before me that the horror had left a mark. If the thought came to him that every one of those tens of thousands whose bodies dammed and reddened the flood was dear to someone weeping in Germany, his eyes gave no sign of it. Perhaps it was as well for the time being. Who knows?

I felt the same revolt against the effect of war when he told me of the taking and losing of Charleroi and set it down as the most "grotesque" sight he had ever seen. "Grotesque" simply made me shudder, when he went on to say that even there, in the narrow streets, the Germans pushed on in "close order," and that the French mitrailleuses, which swept the street that he saw, made such havoc in their ranks that the air was so full of flying heads and arms and legs, of boots, and helmets, swords, and guns that it did not seem as if it could be real—"it looked like some burlesque"; and that even one of the gunners turned ill and said to his commander, who stood beside him: "For the love of God, colonel, shall I go on?" and the colonel, with folded arms, replied: "Fire away."

Perhaps it is lucky, since war is, that men can be like that. When they cannot, what then? But it was too terrible for me, and I changed the subject by asking him if it were true that the Germans deliberately fired on the Red Cross. He instantly became grave and prudent.

"Oh, well," he said, "I would not like to go on oath. We have had our field ambulance destroyed. But you know the Germans are often bad marksmen. They've got an awful lot of ammunition. They fire it all over the place. They are bound to hit something. If we screen our hospital behind a building and a shell comes over and blows us up, how can we swear the shell was aimed at us?"

Just here the regiment came over the hill, and I retreated inside the gate where I had pails of water ready for them to drink. They were a sorry-looking lot. It was a hot day. They were covered with dirt, and you know the ill-fitting uniform of the French common soldier would disfigure into trampdom the best-looking man in the world.

The barricade was still across the road. With

their packs on their backs, their tin dippers in
their hands for the drink they so needed, per-
spiring in their heavy coats, they crawled, line
after line, under the barrier until an officer rode
down and called sharply:

"Halt!"

The line came to a standstill.

"What's that thing?" asked the officer
sternly.

I replied that obviously it was a barricade.

"Who put it there?" he asked peremptorily,
as if I were to blame.

I told him that the English did.

"When?"

I felt as if I were being rather severely cross-
examined, but I answered as civilly as I could,
"The night before the battle."

He looked at me for the first time—and
softened his tone a bit—my white hair and
beastly accent, I suppose—as he asked:

"What is it for?"

I told him it *was* to prevent a detachment of
Uhlans from coming up the hill. He hesitated
a moment; then asked if it served any purpose
now. I might have told him that the Uhlans
were still here, but I didn't, I simply said that I
did not know that it did. "Cut it down!" he
ordered, and in a moment it was cut at one end
and swung round against the bank and the
regiment marched on.

It was just after that that I discovered the

explanation of what had happened to my Irish
scout on Saturday. An exhausted soldier was in
need of a stimulant, and one of his comrades,
who was supporting him, asked me if I had
anything. I had nothing but the bottle out of
which the Irish scout had drunk. I rushed for it,
poured some into the tin cup held out to me,
and just as the poor fellow was about to drink,
his comrade pulled the cup away, smelt it, and
exclaimed, "Don't drink that—here, put some
water in it. That's not cyder. It's *eau de vie des
prunes*."

I can tell you I was startled. I had never
tasted *eau de vie des prunes*—a native brew,
stronger than brandy, and far more dangerous—
and my Irishman had pulled off a full champagne
glass at a gulp, and never winked. No wonder
he fell off his wheel. The wonder is that he did
not die on the spot. I *was* humiliated. Still, he
was Irish and perhaps he didn't care. I hope he
didn't. But only think, he will never know that
I did not do it on purpose. He was probably
gloriously drunk. Anyway, it prevented his
coming back to make that visit he threatened me
with.

The detachment of the regiment which staggered past my gate camped in the fields below
me and in the courtyards at Voisins, and the
rest of them made themselves comfortable in the
fields at the other side of the hill and the outbuildings on Amélie's place, and the officers

and the ambulance corps began to seek their quarters.

I was sitting in the library when my guest, Chef-Major W——, rode up to the gate. I had a good chance to look him over, as he marched up the path. He was a dapper, upright, little chap. He was covered with dust from his head to his heels. I could have written his name on him anywhere. Then I went to the door to meet him. I suppose he had been told that he was to be lodged in the house of an American. He stopped abruptly, half-way up the path, as I appeared, clicked his heels together, and made me his best bow, as he said:

"I am told, madame, that you are so gracious as to offer me a bed."

I might have replied literally, "Offer? I had no choice," but I did not. I said politely that if Monsieur le Chef-Major would take the trouble to enter, I should do myself the distinguished honour of conducting him to his chamber, having no servant for the moment to perform for him that service, and he bowed at me again, and marched in—no other word for it—and came up the stairs behind me.

As I opened the door of my guest-room, and stood aside to let him pass, I found that he had paused half-way up and was giving my raftered green salon and the library beyond a curious glance. Being caught, he looked up at once and said: "So you are not afraid?" I supposed he

was inspired by the fact that there were no signs
of any preparations to evacuate.

I replied that I could not exactly say that, but
that I had not been sufficiently afraid to run
away and leave my house to be looted unless I
had to.

"Well," he said, with a pleasant laugh, "that
is about as good an account of himself as many
a brave soldier can give the night before his first
battle"; and he passed me with a bow and I
closed the door.

Half an hour later he came downstairs, all
shaved and slicked up—in a white sweater,
white tennis shoes, with a silk handkerchief
about his neck, and a fatigue cap set rakishly
on the side of his head, as if there were no such
thing as hot weather or war, while his orderly
went up and brought his equipment down to the
terrace, and began such a beating, brushing, and
cleaning of boots as you never saw.

At the library door he stopped, looked in, and
said, "This is nice"; and before I could get
together decent French enough to say that I was
honoured—or my house was—at his approval,
he asked if he might be so indiscreet as to take
the liberty of inviting some of his fellow officers
to come into the garden and see the view.
Naturally I replied that Monsieur le Chef-Major
was at home and his comrades would be welcome
to treat the garden as if it were theirs, and he
made me another of his bows and marched away,

to return in five minutes, accompanied by half-a-dozen officers and a priest. As they passed the window, where I still sat, they all bowed at me solemnly, and Chef-Major W—— stopped to ask if madame would be so good as to join them, and explain the country, which was new to them all.

Naturally madame did not wish to. I had not been out there since Saturday night—was it less than forty-eight hours before? But equally naturally I was ashamed to refuse. It would, I knew, seem super-sentimental to them. So I reluctantly followed them out. They stood in a group about me—these men who had been in battles, come out safely, and were again advancing to the firing line as smilingly as one would go into a ball-room—while I pointed out the towns and answered their questions, and no one was calmer or more keenly interested than the Breton priest, in his long soutane with the red cross on his arm. All the time the cannon was booming in the north-east, but they paid no more attention to it than if it were a threshing-machine.

There was a young lieutenant in the group who finally noticed a sort of reluctance on my part—which I evidently had not been able to conceal—to looking off at the plain, which I own I had been surprised to find as lovely as ever. He taxed me with it, and I confessed, upon which he said :—

"That will pass. The day will come—Nature

is so made, luckily—when you will look off there with pride, not pain, and be glad that you saw what may prove the turning of the tide in the noblest war ever fought for civilization."

I wonder.

The chef-major turned to me—caught me looking in the other direction—to the west, where deserted Esbly climbed the hill.

" May I be very indiscreet?" he asked.

I told him that he knew best.

" Well," he said, " I want to know how it happens that you—a foreigner, and a woman— happen to be living in what looks like exile—all alone on the top of a hill—in war-time?"

I looked at him a moment—and—well, conditions like these make people friendly with one another at once. I was, you know, never very reticent, and in days like these even the ordinary reticences of ordinary times are swept away. So I answered frankly, as if these men were old friends, and not the acquaintances of an hour, that, as I was, as they could see, no longer young, very tired, and yet not weary with life, but more interested than my strength allowed, I had sought a pleasant retreat for my old age,— not too far from the city of my love,—and that I had chosen this hilltop for the sake of the panorama spread out before me; that I had loved it every day more than the day before; and that exactly three months after I had sat down on this hilltop this awful war had marched

to within sight of my gate, and banged its
cannon and flung its deadly bombs right under
my eyes.

Do you know, every mother's son of them
threw back his head—and laughed aloud. I was
startled. I knew that I had shown unnecessary
feeling—but I knew it too late. I made a dash
for the house, but the lieutenant blocked the
way. I could not make a scene. I never felt so
like it in my life.

"Come back, come back," he said. "We all
apologize. It was a shame to laugh. But you
are so vicious and so personal about it. After
all, you know, the gods were kind to you—it
*did* turn back—those waves of battle. You had
better luck than Canute."

"Besides," said the chef-major, "you can
always say that you had front row stage box."

There was nothing to do to save my face but
to laugh with them. And they were still laughing when they tramped across the road to dinner.
I returned to the house rather mortified at
having been led into such an unnecessary display
of feeling, but I suppose I had been in need of
some sort of an outlet.

After dinner they came back to the lawn to
lie about smoking their cigarettes. I was sitting in the arbour. The battle had become a
duel of heavy artillery, which they all found
"magnificent," these men who had been in such
things.

Suddenly the chef-major leaped to his feet.

" Listen—listen—an aeroplane."

We all looked up. There it was, quite low, right over our heads.

"A Taube!" he exclaimed, and before he had got the words out of his mouth, *Crick-crack-crack* snapped the musketry from the field behind us—the soldiers had seen it. The machine began to rise. I stood like a rock,—my feet glued to the ground,—while the regiment fired over my head. But it was sheer will power that kept me steady among these men who were treating it as if it were a Fourteenth of July show. I heard a *ping*.

" Touched," said the officer as the Taube continued to rise. Another *ping*. Still it rose, and we watched it sail off towards the hills at the south-east.

"Hit, but not hurt," sighed the officer, dropping down on the grass again, with a sigh. "It is hard to bring them down at that height, with rifles, but it can be done."

"Perhaps the English battery will get it," said I; "It is going right toward it."

"If there is an English battery up there," replied he, "that is probably what he is looking for. It is hardly likely to unmask for a Taube. I am sorry we missed it. You have seen something of the war. It is a pity you should not have seen it come down. It is a beautiful sight."

I thought to myself that I preferred it should not come down in my garden. But I had no relish for being laughed at again, so I did not say it.

Soon after they all went to bed,—very early, —and silence fell on the hilltop. I took a look round before I went to bed. I had not seen Amélie since the regiment arrived. But she, who had done everything to spare me inconvenience, had fourteen officers quartered in her place, and goodness knows how many horses, so she had little time to do for me.

The hillside was a picture I shall never forget. Everywhere men were sleeping in the open— their guns beside them. Fires, over which they had cooked, were smouldering; pickets everywhere. The moon shed a pale light and made long shadows. It was really very beautiful if one could have forgotten that to-morrow many of these men would be sleeping for good— "Life's fitful dream" over.

# XVI

THIS morning everything and everybody
was astir early. It was another gloriously
beautiful day. The birds were singing as if to
split their throats. There was a smell of coffee
all over the place. Men were hurrying up and
down the hill, to and fro from the wash-house,
bathing, washing out their shirts and stockings
and hanging them on the bushes, rubbing down
horses and douching them, cleaning saddles and
accoutrements. There is a lot of work to be
done by an army besides fighting. It was all
like a play, and everyone was so cheerful.

The chef-major did not come down until his
orderly called him, and when he did he looked
as rosy and cheerful as a child, and announced
that he had slept like one. Soon after he crossed
the road for his coffee I heard the officers laughing and chatting as if it were a week-end house
party.

When Amélie came to get my breakfast she
looked a wreck—I saw one of her famous bilious
attacks coming.

It was a little after eleven, while the chef-
major was upstairs writing, that his orderly came

with a paper and carried it up to him. He came down at once, made me one of his pretty bows at the door of the library, and holding out a scrap of paper said :—

"Well, madame, we are going to leave you. We advance at two."

I asked him where he was going.

He glanced at the paper in his hand, and replied :—

"Our orders are to advance to Saint-Fiacre,— a little east of Meaux,—but before I go I am happy to relieve your mind on two points. The French cavalry has driven the Uhlans out—some of them were captured as far east as Bouleurs. And the English artillery has come down from the hill behind you and is crossing the Marne. We follow them. So you see you can sit here in your pretty library and read all these nice books in security, until the day comes—perhaps sooner than you dare hope—when you can look back to all these days, and perhaps be a little proud to have had a small part in it" ; and off he went upstairs.

I sat perfectly still for a long time. Was it possible that it was only a week ago that I had heard the drum beat for the disarming of the Seine et Marne? Was there really going to come a day when all the beauty around me would not be a mockery? All at once it occurred to me that I had promised Captain S—— to write and tell him how I had "come through." Perhaps this was the time. I went to the foot of the stairs and called up to the chef-major. He came to the door and I explained, asking him if, we being without a post-office, he could get a letter through, and what kind of a letter I could write, as I knew the censorship was severe.

"My dear Lady," he replied, "go and write your letter,—write anything you like,—and when I come down I will take charge of it and guarantee that it shall go through, uncensored, no matter what it contains."

So I wrote to tell Captain S—— that all was well at Huiry,—that we had escaped, and were still grateful for all the trouble he had taken. When the officer came down I gave it to him, unsealed.

"Seal it, seal it," he said, and when I had done so, he wrote, "Read and approved" on the envelope, and gave it to his orderly, and was ready to say "Good-bye."

"Don't look so serious about it," he laughed, as we shook hands. "Some of us will get killed, but what of that? I wanted this war. I prayed for it. I should have been sad enough if I had died before it came. I have left a wife and children whom I adore, but I am ready to lay down my life cheerfully for the victory of which I am so sure. Cheer up. I think my hour has not yet come. I had three horses killed under me in Belgium. At Charleroi a bomb exploded in a staircase as I was coming down. I jumped—

not a scratch to show. Things like that make a man feel immune—but who knows?"

I did my best to smile, as I said, "I don't wish you courage—you have that, but—good luck."

"Thank you," he replied, "you've had that"; and away he marched, and that was the last I saw of him.

I had a strange sensation about these men who had in so few days passed so rapidly in and out of my life, and in a moment seemed like old friends.

There was a bustle of preparation all about us. Such a harnessing of horses, such a rolling-up of half-dried shirts, but it was all orderly and systematic. Over it all hung a smell of soup-kettles—the preparations for the midday meal, and a buzz of many voices as the men sat about eating out of their tin dishes. I did wish I could see only the picturesque side of it.

It was two o'clock sharp when the regiment began to move. No bands played. No drum beat. They just marched, marched, marched along the road to Meaux, and silence fell again on the hill-side.

Off to the north-east the cannon still boomed, —it is still booming now as I write, and it is after nine o'clock. There has been no sign of Amélie all day as I have sat here writing all this to you. I have tried to make it as clear a statement of facts as I could. I am afraid that I have been more disturbed in putting it down than I was in living it. Except on Saturday and Sunday I was always busy, a little useful, and that helped. I don't know when I shall be able to get this off to you. But at least it is ready, and I shall take the first opportunity I get to cable to you, as I am afraid before this you have worried, unless your geography is faulty, and the American papers as reticent as ours.

THE END

CHISWICK PRESS : PRINTED BY CHARLES WHITTINGHAM AND CO. TOOKS COURT, CHANCERY LANE, LONDON.